D1409536

"This series is the answer to the cry of my heart. It's wise, it's tactical, and it's preemptive. Among the huge selection of parenting books on my shelf, I've never had another one give me tingles and make me shout, 'Yes! This is it!' I feel empowered and inspired as a parent and have already implemented the strategies this series teaches."

—Jill Williamson, Christy Award–winning author of *By Darkness Hid* and the Blood of Kings trilogy

"Nicole O'Dell has created something that is—in my opinion—revolutionary in helping parents of teens. The idea of creating scenarios prior to issues arising and then coming alongside our teens to help them navigate those scenarios is going to help me a ton! My only regret is that I didn't read this book sooner! If you are a parent, pick this book up. It will make you think differently about how you communicate with your kids!"

—Marybeth Whalen, Proverbs 31 Ministries writer and speaker, author of *The Mailbox* and *She Makes It Look Easy*

FRANKLIN COUNTY LIBRARY SYSTEM
101 RAGGED EDGE ROAD SOUTH
CHAMBERSBURG, PA 17202

GROVE FAMILY LIBRARY
101 RAGGED EDGE ROAD SOUTH
CHAMBERSBURG, PA 17202

Hot Buttons Series

Hot Buttons Internet Edition
Hot Buttons Dating Edition

Releasing Fall 2012

Hot Buttons Drug Edition
Hot Buttons Sexuality Edition

HOT BUTTONS

INTERNET EDITION

Nicole O'Dell

Kregel
Publications

Hot Buttons Internet Edition
Copyright © 2012 by Nicole O'Dell

Published by Kregel Publications, a division of Kregel, Inc., P.O. Box 2607, Grand Rapids, MI 49501.

All rights reserved. No part of this book may be reproduced, stored in a retrieval system, or transmitted in any form or by any means—electronic, mechanical, photocopy, recording, or otherwise—without written permission of the publisher, except for brief quotations in printed reviews.

The authors and publisher are not engaged in rendering medical or psychological services, and this book is not intended as a guide to diagnose or treat medical or psychological problems. If medical, psychological, or other expert assistance is required by the reader, please seek the services of your own physician or certified counselor.

All Scripture quotations, unless otherwise indicated, are taken from the Holy Bible, New International Version®, NIV®. Copyright © 1973, 1978, 1984, 2011 by Biblica, Inc.™ Used by permission of Zondervan. All rights reserved worldwide. www.zondervan.com

Scripture quotations marked NASB are taken from the New American Standard Bible®. Copyright © 1960, 1962, 1963, 1968, 1971, 1972, 1973, 1975, 1977, 1995 by The Lockman Foundation. Used by permission. www.Lockman.org

Scripture quotations marked NKJV are from the New King James Version®. Copyright © 1982 by Thomas Nelson, Inc. Used by permission. All rights reserved.

Library of Congress Cataloging-in-Publication Data
O'Dell, Nicole.
Hot buttons / Nicole O'Dell. — Internet ed.
   p.   cm. — (Hot buttons series)
Includes bibliographical references (p.   ).
1. Parenting—Religious aspects—Christianity.   2. Child rearing—Religious aspects—Christianity.
3. Internet—Religious aspects—Christianity.   4. Christian teenagers—Conduct of life.   I. Title.
BV4529.O343   2012   248.8'45—dc23   2012003661

ISBN 978-0-8254-4239-1

Printed in the United States of America
12 13 14 15 16 / 5 4 3 2 1

The Hot Buttons series, as a whole, is dedicated to my mom who had to deal with more hot buttons when I was a teen than she'd care to remember. Also to my six children who have so graciously provided the research I needed to write these books . . . whether I wanted them to or not. And to my husband, Wil, who somehow managed to make my teen years look like a walk in the park.

Hot Buttons Internet Edition *is dedicated to my writer-sisters: Jenny B. Jones, Cara Putman, Kim Cash Tate, Cindy Thomson, Marybeth Whalen, and Kit Wilkinson. Your sisterhood is proof that the Internet can be a wonderful place.*

Love you all!

>>> *When I was a boy of fourteen, my father was so ignorant I could hardly stand to have the old man around. But when I got to be twenty-one, I was astonished at how much he had learned in seven years.*

—MARK TWAIN

Contents

Part Four: Parent-Teen Study Guide

Preface

Years ago, when I was searching for ways to lead my children to make good decisions, I decided it would be far better to talk to them proactively about issues they would one day face than it would be to wait until they were buried under the consequences of their poor choices. I believed it would be far easier to guide the way they perceived the information and to help them understand the consequences of poor decisions if they could look at them objectively, without the added stress of peer pressure and other outside influences. I needed a safe way to talk with my kids about things like sex, drugs, alcohol, addictions, dating, pornography, Internet use, and other hot-button issues—perhaps even before they actually knew what those things were.

So, I devised a game I called Scenarios.

I would give my kids a scenario as though it were a situation they were facing at the moment. It ended with a choice they had to make between three or four options, which I spelled out to them. I made sure they felt safe in choosing any option—even if it was clearly the wrong one. This was a learning exercise, and I much preferred that my kids make their mistakes within the safety of a dining room discussion rather than in a less forgiving environment.

The practice of Scenarios became a favorite activity in my home and proved invaluable in preparing my teens to make good choices. The best parts were the talks we'd have after the choices were made and the consequences were presented. They felt free to explore, ask questions, and experiment safely with the options—and then, when similar scenarios came up in real life, they were prepared to make the right choices.

The Hot Buttons series was birthed as a way for you to bring the principles and practices of my family's Scenarios game into your home. This book deals with Internet activity, online access, and the various dangers lurking in the cyber world. When you start to delve into these issues, you're going to see the threat in every direction. Ultimately, God is in control, but you are His ambassador in your home.

In part 1, I will cover the idea of confronting hot-button issues in general—why, when, and how you should take a preemptive stand. Some parents may feel that ten or eleven years old is too young to start talking openly with tweens about things like pornography or sex trafficking. These introductory chapters will explain why I vehemently disagree.

In part 2, I detail various hot-button issues to help you understand the specifics of each Internet hot button your kids will face. Each chapter of this section includes warning signs to watch for and recommended action steps to take right away.

In part 3, I give you everything you need to start pressing the hot buttons and proactively preparing your teens to make good choices. It's in this section that you will find Strategic Scenarios to work through with your kids. These Strategic Scenarios will enable you to approach these hot-button topics and give your kids the same opportunity to make safe discoveries that I gave to my kids—and I trust you'll see the same results I have.

In part 4, you'll have the opportunity to identify the specific Internet hot buttons in your home, reverse mistakes, and do the work to repair any damage that may have already been done. Then you'll be prompted to make a plan to avoid those dangers in the future. You'll also be walked through the dual processes of confession and forgiveness, both within your family and in your relationship with God.

One thing you'll notice about each Hot Buttons book is that they're all structured in the same way. Some of the content is reiterated with subtle changes to direct it to the issue being discussed. This similarity is intentional. The truth of God's Word doesn't change, and the importance of good decisions is universal. The Bible is clear and effective—and speaks for itself. I recommend that you work through the parent-teen study guide for each book, even if you've done it before. The Lord will show you new things as you approach His Word for answers on each new hot-button issue.

The Hot Buttons books are designed to serve as manuals for those tough, preemptive discussions you need to have with your children. My goal is that you'll be able to pick up any edition and use it as a learning and teaching tool to prepare yourself and your kids to face potential dangers. Then when a specific hot-button issue pops up in the future, you can come back to the appropriate edition and use it as a quick-reference guide.

These books (and other tools and resources out there) are great ways to tackle the tough issues our kids face, but nothing is more effective than prayer and communication. I pray that you'll use the Hot Buttons books as steps leading you to better communication with the Father through prayer and with your teens through open dialogue.

Acknowledgments

Wil, Erik, Natalie, Emily, Logan, Megan, and Ryleigh. I'm so in love with you people. Thanks for loving me back and supporting me on this journey.

I want to thank Diana Sharples and Jill Williamson for their invaluable, rapid-fire critiques of this book and their feedback on the Hot Buttons concept as a whole. Jill, the changes you've already made to your own online presence in response to this book are tangible proof that the words sank in. Thanks to you both for your eyes, ears, prayers, and friendship!

My writer-sisters: Jenny Jones, Cara Putman, Kim Cash Tate, Cindy Thomson, Marybeth Whalen, and Kit Wilkinson. You guys are my heart . . . my partners in writing, and in life. I am so thankful to God for your humor, your prayers, your support, and even the occasional, "Are you crazy?!"

Valerie Comer, the sounding board of your mind is where many of my ideas are fleshed out. I so appreciate your never-ending questions and challenges that pull the best of me out from somewhere in there. When I'm satisfied with good enough, you make me reach for more. And funny enough, you're another one who shouts a well-deserved, "Are you crazy?!" on a semi-regular basis.

Chip MacGregor, literary agent extraordinaire, thanks for not telling me I'm crazy, even when you think it. Thanks for helping me navigate the rough waters of the publishing industry, and for having faith in me.

And, lastly, I'm forever thankful to God for His redemptive power and His forgiveness. Without those two things, I'd have no authority to write this book.

PART ONE

Internet
HOT
BUTTONS

What exactly is a hot-button issue? A *hot button* is any emotional or controversial issue that has the potential to trigger intense reaction. What topics jump to mind that fit this description when you think of teens and tweens? Pretty much everything that pummels your kids with temptation and threatens to pull them away from a walk with God. Music, dating, computer use, texting, partying . . . The list goes on. Moms and Dads, these issues are real and often confusing. They require attention—*before* they arise. Ignoring them can have dire consequences that our children will have to live with for the rest of their lives. The decision to just wait until an actual situation arises before we face a subject is naive, at best, and possibly lethal. We have both a parental right and a godly responsibility to hit these issues hard, head-on. If we approach them preemptively, our teens will be prepared to face and handle life's toughest battles.

Prepared:
Answering *Why*

It is surprising how little power many parents exercise over the lives of their teens. In so many homes, the teens are in charge. They use manipulation tactics, bad attitudes, arguments, and even threats to get their way. They play on parents' fears and weaknesses, and they know just when to strike and how far is too far. Parents throw their hands up in the air and surrender the fight. Their lukewarm tactics become about surviving, not thriving. They figure they only have to endure the trial of the teen years for a short time and, if they can just get through this season, things will be better.

Mom, Dad, if that's your attitude, please think about how that sounds. You're basically saying you aren't going to worry about what your teens do or think, and you're just going to hope and pray that you all reach their adulthood with as few proverbial bruises as possible. I beg you to rethink the teen years. Where infancy was training for toddlerhood, and childhood was preparation for the teen years, the teen years are the foundation for adulthood. It's during these most important years that your teenager will:

- prepare to choose a mate
- establish financial habits
- develop a work ethic
- cultivate parenting skills
- grow into—or out of—a deeper personal relationship with God

The teen years are an extremely important preparation time! And, parents, it's time to stand up and make these years count. You don't need to *get* through these years; you need to *power* through them. Take charge, and make a difference.

I'm not advocating for a take-no-prisoners attitude in our homes, however. Our children need to feel love, not condemnation. They should trust that we're an ally, not the enemy. You're not fighting *against* your kids in hopes of coming out victorious over them; you're in a battle *for* them.

> For our struggle is **not against flesh and blood**, but against the rulers, against the authorities, against the powers of this dark world and **against the spiritual forces of evil** in the heavenly realms. (Eph. 6:12)

Dispel the myth of effective insulation.

Let's face it. If we're raising our kids as Christians, they're at a huge disadvantage by the world's standards. The world assumes that teenagers from churchgoing, Christ-following homes are socially underdeveloped, behind the times physically and emotionally, and uneducated in worldly matters like politics, public issues, pretty much everything in the news.

As Christian parents we try to insulate our families from negative outside influences; we keep watch over the things that enter their young minds through television, movies, language, peer pressure, and the Internet. Our goal is not to render them unsavvy but to shield them from the wiles of the enemy. Then things that are seemingly innocuous, like social media, come along and swallow our families whole.

Don't you wish we could walk with our kids through the battles of life—guarding and guiding them through each pressure-filled moment, each decision between right and wrong, each temptation? While God-honoring parents absolutely should have high expectations and maintain a tight grip on the reins as they raise their families, we also need to prepare our kids to stand alone.

You can't control what the world throws at them, but you can affect how prepared they are to defend themselves against the onslaught. In each and every pressure-filled moment of decision, there comes a point just before the final decision is made, a point when all the preparation, forethought, and wisdom we've been equipping our kids with comes to a head. Once the hot button is pushed, the opportunity for laying groundwork is over; in the heat of the moment there's no time for anything else, and they make a choice based on all the work that came before. Our teens need to be equipped to make the right choice; armed with something more than *no*; braced by facts, your wisdom, and God's Word.

Teens will likely face persecution, disappointment, and even out-and-out rejection when they choose to stand for what's right. If we're proactive, our children can reach their teen years already armed with the tools necessary to make hard choices in the face of those afflictions—willing to withstand and endure them for the sake of Christ and for their own well-being.

Prepared: Answering *Why*

Take the mystery out of sin!

If you were to start a new job as a police officer, you'd have to go through a lot of training first, right? They aren't going to just hand you a gun and give you keys to a squad car, then send you out into the community to learn as you go.

You'd be trained to recognize the signs of danger and respond to them with strength and confidence. You'd be given tools to help you remain in control in various situations. You'd understand the power of your weapons and how to use them appropriately. And you'd be trained to stand firm in the face of any kind of threat.

In Mark 14:38, we're warned to watch and pray about temptation. Even for Christian adults, our spirits are willing to avoid temptation, but we are cautioned to be attentive because our bodies are weak. How much more so for someone who isn't prepared for temptation! We may have raised the most well-intentioned kids on the planet—ones whose spirits are willing—but their flesh is weak. They need to be trained.

> **Fix these words of mine in your hearts and minds**; tie them as symbols on your hands and bind them on your foreheads. **Teach them to your children**, talking about them when you sit at home and when you walk along the road, when you lie down and when you get up. (Deut. 11:18–19)

We may wish we lived in a Christian bubble, but pretending we do so ignores a huge need. It results in teens who are sent out into the world unarmed and unprepared for situations they can't avoid. Our kids will face temptation, peer pressure, and sinful desires; it's a fact. Why not arm them with understanding and preparation? It's more important to prepare your children than it is to attempt to create a sterile, sin-free environment in a world that makes it impossible.

Through the knowledge and application of God's Word and the pursuit of His will through advanced preparation, today's youth need to be committed to safe Internet practices before they ever approach a computer. Ephesians 6:13 says, "Put on the full armor of God, so that when the day of evil comes, you may be able to stand your ground, and after you have done everything, to stand." (In chapter 10, we're going to do just that as it pertains to your teens and the Internet.)

Parents can help their kids achieve the level of advanced preparation they'll need to stand by

◀ helping them figure out why they should care;
◀ giving them the tools they need to succeed; and
◀ walking them through the process of making good choices.

Why should they care? What's in it for them if they stand on God's Word in the face of peer pressure, risking friendships, popularity, good times? Our teens need to believe that the Lord has a plan for them and His ways are best. The most effective ways to instill those beliefs are to model them and teach them. A time-invested parent, who prays as much as she talks and listens as much as she prays, will have the best chance of raising a child eager and willing to say NO and mean it.

What tools do they need? Our teens and preteens need options. A busy life with wholesome things like church activities and sports—alternatives to the negatives. They need to be a part of a family that is serving the Lord, and they need to be watching parents who practice what they preach. They need to continuously grow in the knowledge of the Word and in relationship with God.

How can they walk through this? They need you to walk with them, hand in hand, step by step. Mom, Dad, Guardian—they need you to be aware of what's going on. They need you to know them well. This requires time, communication, and godly insight into the minds of your teens.

We can be confident parents, even in these scary times!

Today's choices have such far-reaching and permanent consequences for our kids, it's hard to trust that everything will just work out fine in the end. Some of our teens' decisions will affect the rest of their lives. Knowing that they're ill-equipped to make those choices, it's very difficult not to panic. It would be easier to lock them up for a few years and check in at, oh, around twenty-two.

We do have a promise to cling to, though.

> **Being confident of this**, that he who began a good work in you will carry it on to completion **until the day of Christ Jesus**. (Phil. 1:6)

Let's break that down.

Being confident of this:
You can be sure that this is the way it is. It's a promise.

He who began:
Who began it? "He" did. Not you. Not your teen. God started . . .

A good work:
The work He started is a good and righteous thing.

Will carry it on to completion:
It will be finished. He didn't start something only to see it fall to pieces because of some teenage mistakes. It *will* be completed. It's a promise of God, and I choose to believe Him.

Until the day of Christ Jesus:
Here's the thing, though. Every one of us, including our teens, is a work in progress. This work, which will be completed, has a long way to go . . . until the day of Christ Jesus, to be exact.

The battle we fight in protecting, shielding, and preparing our teens for life's hot-button issues isn't as black-and-white as a physical battle in which the wins and losses can be easily quantified. We must often blindly face the battles for our kids, operating more on faith than on sight, being obedient to the call of Christ and reliant on the leading of the Holy Spirit. We have been given tools in God's Word to prepare us to guard against the confusion of this world, however. And we're granted partnership with the Holy Spirit, who will lead and guide us according to godly wisdom and sight. That guidance is invaluable as we prepare our kids for life's battles.

CHECK POINTS

✓ It's time to stand up and make these years count. You don't need to *get* through these years; you need to *power* through them.

✓ The battle we fight is not *against* our teens, it's *for* them!

✓ "For our struggle is not against flesh and blood, but against the rulers, against the authorities, against the powers of this dark world and against the spiritual forces of evil in the heavenly realms. Therefore put on the full armor of God, so that when the day of evil comes, you may be able to stand your ground, and after you have done everything, to stand" (Eph. 6:12–13).

✓ Today's youth need to be committed to safe Internet practices before they ever approach a computer.

✓ A time-invested parent, who prays as much as she talks and listens as much as she prays, has the best chance of raising a child eager and willing to say NO and mean it.

✓ We cannot wait until our teens come face-to-face with peer pressure and expect them to know how to handle something they aren't prepared for.

Watchful:
Answering *When*

You may be thinking, "I'll just wait until these issues surface and then I'll talk with my kids about how to handle them." In reality, you have to be willing to tackle tough issues openly and honestly before they actually come up. That might feel uncomfortable—like you're giving your preteen or teenager too much information, too soon. But you'll see why that's not the case as you work through the Hot Buttons books. Information about life's tough issues needs to come from you—in a controlled, intentional way—rather than from their peers. This is the core message of the Hot Buttons series.

These days, young people are forced to make adult decisions long before we think they'll have to and long before they're ready. Since we weren't expecting the issues to come up so soon and they had no idea what was looming on their horizon, they inevitably make mistakes out of plain and simple lack of foresight. We need to help them predetermine what their choices are going to be, because in the heat of the moment, they won't be able to sort through all the factors about an issue they haven't prepared for. At those times, it's far easier to just give in to peer pressure than to come up with the right alternative and be strong enough to live it out.

The world is doing everything it can to deflect your kids' attention, allegiance, and affection away from God; and the Internet has, in most cases, successfully won your kids' attention, allegiance, and affection. Through this medium and others, the world throws temptation and sin in your kids' faces when they are incredibly young, so you need to go after the tough issues even earlier than you think. If your son is going to open a social networking account when he's thirteen, he needs to learn about the risks and dangers and develop a plan for avoiding them when he's twelve. If your daughter is going to be pressured to share photos online at fourteen, she needs to understand the dangers by the time she's thirteen. If she's going to be approached by a predator on the Internet, she needs to know what rape, murder, and sex trafficking are, and why strangers on the Internet put her at risk for victimization. Pretending those things don't exist or avoiding them for too long dangles your teen over a cliff. Are you willing to take a chance that he or she won't fall headfirst?

If you wait until your teens come face-to-face with issues and then expect them to know how to handle something they aren't prepared for . . . well, it just might be too late. Even if they're willing for you to rescue them *after* the fact—and that's by no means a sure thing—what about saving them from falling in the first place?

What don't your kids want you to know?

Honestly, kids don't want *you* to know what *they* know about various issues. If you're in the dark and think they are too—golden! This doesn't mean that they want to rebel or are hiding horrible things, but they don't want to admit that they're mentally exploring ideas and possibilities of the things they're discovering. Eventually—maybe after a long time or maybe after hardly any time at all—a thought will turn into action. That's why it's vital, Mom and Dad, that you're educated about what your teens are exposed to, armed with the tools to guide them, and then ready to stand watch.

If you haven't initiated conversations about these issues, it's highly unlikely that your teenager is going to run to you with her cell phone and show you a sexy message or picture she received, or that your son will show you the Facebook pictures of the girls who are flirting with him. But these kinds of secrets are when the erosion starts.

Those first flirts with danger, the first tempting sin—if it goes well—makes way for more and more. The only way to prevent that is with information and awareness.

How early is too early?

Many parents fear that if they approach certain topics too early, it will give their kids ideas about those things before they actually need to face them.

Let me ask you some questions:

- ◀ Do your children ride the school bus with older students?
- ◀ Are there older kids in your neighborhood?
- ◀ Do your children know how to use the remote control?
- ◀ Do your kids ever watch TV when you're not in the room?

- Do you exercise a double standard by watching or allowing television programs or movies that depict things you're supposedly against?
- Are your kids allowed to watch PG movies?
- Do they have access to the Internet at home or at school?
- Is there ever unsupervised Internet access in your home?
- Do they have memberships to social media networks?
- Do they have memberships to social sites that you don't know how to check up on?

If you answered yes to any of those questions—even one—your concern shouldn't be whether it's too early to address this hot button, but rather if it's *too late* for the kind of preemptive action I'm talking about. If you answered yes, then the chances are you need to begin taking a bit more of a *reactive* approach—which is equally necessary.

Don't misunderstand me. I'm not saying that all of those things in the list above are necessarily bad things, but they are open doors that expose your kids to issues that you need to address. *Now*.

Just because you don't use swear words in your house, for example, you can't pretend your kids don't hear them on the school bus. My oldest daughter had learned all of them from the older kids on the bus long before it occurred to me that she might know them. You may shield your tweens from talk of dating and teen relationships, but what about the eleventh graders making out in the back of the bus? You might supervise Internet activity, but what about the computers at friends' houses or the hacker at school who knows too much and likes to show off?

How old is old enough?

Everyone is different. Some tweens are early bloomers and are far more advanced and aware than others of the same age. Then there are those who prefer to hang back in their innocence a little longer. In general, kids surrounded by older teens discover and experiment at a faster rate than those who are not.

Physical and emotional changes often go hand in hand, but not always at the same rate. There is a clear distinction between puberty and adolescence. *Puberty* is physical. The effects are ones we can witness as maturing bodies transform. These changes start at different times for each individual and span several years.

The changes of *adolescence*, however, are more emotional and mental. Even though the physical adjustments suggest that emotional changes are imminent, they don't always go right along the same path or speed. It's the hidden, stealthy nuances that you need to watch out for.

Changes that signal adolescence:

> - dramatic change in behavior
> - separating or distancing from parents, adults, and/or other family members
> - showing more independence from Mom and Dad
> - wanting to fit in with peers
> - experimenting with looks and identities
> - discarding childhood treasures, habits, etc.
> - blaming parents
> - being bored with family time

Watchful: Answering *When*

What don't you want your kids to know?

Oh, believe me, I could make a list a mile long of the things I wish my teens didn't know about, and I'm sure you feel the same way. The problem is, your kids will know about all of those things at some point, if they don't already. You need to turn your thinking away from not wanting the knowledge to exist, and get it more focused on not wanting your teens to get curious and *explore* that knowledge on their own.

You don't want your teens to learn by personal experience:
- How the wrong choice feels
- How one mistake leads to another one
- The pain of the aftereffects
- The desire to undo something that can't be erased
- Regret

Can you save them from those things every single time?
- No, probably not.

Is saving them from one mistake worth all of this effort?
- Of course it is.

Let's stop being horrified by the truth about what our teens are faced with and start doing something to equip them to handle it. Pretending it doesn't exist is like not talking about the elephant in the room. Eventually, that elephant is going to get restless and hungry. It's vital that you're educated about what your teens are exposed to, armed with the tools to guide them, and then ready to stand watch.

CHECK POINTS

✓ "Watch and pray so that you will not fall into temptation. The spirit is willing, but the flesh is weak" (Mark 14:38).

✓ Let's stop being horrified by the truth about what our teens are faced with and start doing something to equip them to handle it.

✓ Information about life's tough issues needs to come from you—in a controlled, intentional way—rather than from their peers.

✓ Those first flirts with danger, the first tempting sin—if it goes well—makes way for more and more. The only way to prevent that is with information and awareness.

✓ The physical and emotional changes of adolescence often go hand in hand, but not always at the same rate, so parents must tailor their approach to each individual.

✓ We need to help our kids predetermine what their choices are going to be because they aren't mature enough to think clearly in the heat of the moment. It's far easier, at those times, to just give in under pressure instead of reasoning through to the right alternative.

Proactive:
Answering *How*

chapter 3

The dreaded eye roll. It's every parent's least-favorite expression, and it's the signal of the end of an era. As children make the transition into their teen years, a parent's heroic status slowly erodes. Suddenly, the two people with all the answers to life's most important questions are out of touch and become—horror of horrors—a complete and utter embarrassment.

As it becomes apparent that your kids are entering adolescence, it's necessary to change your tactics. Childhood was a time of learning and discovery, a time when your child looked to you as the supreme teacher and guide. Now it's vital that you adjust your approach by encouraging open, honest, age-appropriate communication—even when the questions are difficult and demand tough answers. It's difficult to make the transitions in accordance with their age, but it's necessary because, believe me, their friends are transitioning too, and along with those changes comes experimentation.

Whatever you do, don't relate.

You'll quickly lose credibility with your teens if you try to pretend you're like them. You're not. This isn't debatable. You're an adult with adult responsibilities, and you're at a place in your life when you're ready to face them. How can a teenager be expected to believe that you're a contemporary, a buddy, a friend? Furthermore, they don't want or need that from you.

Studies have shown that teens feel the most distance from parents who try to be their friends. They have peers at school. At home, they need and want a parent.

Instead of trying to relate and be accepted by your teen as a contemporary, gain credibility by admitting and embracing your differences. Don't subject yourself to the eye roll and the comments about how out of touch you are; admit it yourself. Make it a source of humor between you and your teen. Embrace the generation gap as something to be proud of, not a deep, dark secret.

What Not to Wear

Make your teenager proud by dressing nicely and caring about your appearance. But don't take it so far that you're sharing clothes and trying to fit in with the teenagers. Be confident and stylish, but stay toward the middle of the pack. Trying to be too trendy is as glaring a faux pas as being frumpy and out of touch. Either extreme will be a source of embarrassment and a reason for your daughter or son to feel distanced from you.

Again, teenagers want to know their parents have a handle on life. If you're still floundering for your own identity and fighting to regain your youth, you're going to confuse your kids. Confidence, self-assuredness, and a moderate sense style will make you more of a cool yet dependable parent—a wardrobe straight out of your teen's closet will have the opposite effect.

What Not to Say

Don't adopt words or phrasing you hear your teens and their friends batting around. It just looks like you're trying too hard. My daughter says *uber* and *epic* all the time. But when I joke around and throw one of those words into a sentence, she just rolls her eyes. Why? Because she knows it's not me and that I'm just desperately and pathetically trying to relate to her on a level where she doesn't need me or want me to be.

It's fake and contrived. Teenagers see right through that every single time.

Along with skipping those uberly epic phrases (see what I mean?), you want to think before you relate. Don't throw in a story from your past every time an issue arises. Wait until your teens ask you about your own teen years. A sure path to an eye roll is for you to say, "Oh, I went through the same thing when I was your age."

Avoid:
> ➤ "I can relate."
> ➤ "When I was your age . . ."
> ➤ "Oh, this will pass."
> ➤ "Wait until you have adult problems . . ."
> ➤ Trendy speech
> ➤ Saying that someone else has it worse—that feels impossible to your teen and seems like a brush-off.
> ➤ Trying to convince your son or daughter that this will go away—it's present now, that's all that matters.
> ➤ Belittling the issue—even though teenage problems aren't as big as adult problems, they are the most important thing to your teen in that moment.

> ➤ Laughing—this hardly needs commentary, but it happens so often. Don't tease your teens about their hormone-driven angst.

There are also some key validating phrases that can go a long way toward bridging the gap between you and your teen:

"Wow. I can see why this would be a confusing situation for you."
"Ouch. That must hurt."
"Would you like advice, or do you want me to just listen?"
"That must be so frustrating."

Whatever you do, don't be unapproachable.

Mom, Dad, it's time to shoot straight. What happened the last time your teen approached you to have a chat? Did you even look up from your computer screen, television program, or book before you uttered one of those phrases your teens have learned to hate?

"Uh-huh."
"Sure, whatever."
"Not right now."

When asked what teens don't like about adults, the biggest complaint is that parents don't really listen. They feel dismissed, ignored. Below I've listed some actual responses I received from teens when I asked them that very question:

"They pretend to hear by grunting, nodding, even sort of laughing when they think they should, but offer no real response to show me they even heard what I said."

"They don't ask any questions about what I said. They're too happy I stopped talking and are afraid to 'put another quarter in' [a phrase that parent actually uses]."

"Dad gets mad when I'm confused and just wants to spout out advice and expects me to take it without any further discussion."

"They're 'too busy.'"

"They say things like, 'Give me ten more minutes' or 'Not now, okay?' They aren't exactly rude, but they kind of brush me off."

"I know my mom loves me, but I just wish I could have a little face time for real."

Ouch.

Before you're going to be able to make an impact regarding the hot-button issues in your kid's life, you're going to need to gain his trust. He must believe that you're interested in whatever interests him and cannot ever feel that you're bored by his concerns. And, much worse than feeling that you're bored is feeling that you're uninterested. If your teen feels like you just want him to go away, he will.

You and I both know that pretty much whatever is bothering your teen will pass—maybe the next day or maybe next week. In a year, it will be a dim memory and other issues will have taken center stage. But more important than dealing with the specific issue or solving the immediate problem is to let your teen know that you take her seriously and care enough to listen to whatever it is. The feeling of rejection that comes when parents brush off concerns builds to an unidentifiable resentment that can lead to rebellion and anger.

This is especially true when we're covering the issues that go along with a cyber lifestyle. If you're too busy to look up from your computer screen to spend real time with your teen, you're sending a message that whatever you're finding online is more important. Imagine, then, how your teen will treat unsupervised Internet access. If it can enrapture you, your teen is sure going to find out why the next time the computer's available.

> ▶ ▶ **Challenge:** *The next time your kid walks in the room, close your laptop or turn away from the screen immediately. Be available so it doesn't always have to feel like an interruption just to ask you a question.*

Whatever you do, don't preach.

If raising children were simple, parents would be able to share stories and offer advice, imparting the wisdom they gleaned from their own personal failures and poor decisions. The children would see their parents as interesting, protective, and wise. They would cling to the sage advice and suggestions their parent offered . . . in fact, they would beg for it.

But every parent knows that's just not the way it works. We didn't treat our parents that way (and probably still don't), and our kids won't see us in that light either. Most preteens will pretend to listen just long enough to make Mom and Dad happy, and then blissfully and confidently go their own way, shucking the parental words off their shoulders with each step while they proceed to do whatever they want to do.

Like you and I did.

One of the most difficult things for parents and religious educators to do is to find a way to engage teenagers on a spiritual level over the table of Scripture. We believe wholeheartedly that God's Word, hidden in the hearts of believers, will guide them through life's tough choices and difficult moments. But until our kids have lived through pain and mistakes, until they've had a need to call on the Word of God themselves, it can be difficult to instill that dependency.

In other words, how do we get our teens to care about God's Word *now*, so they are armed and ready later when faced with hot-button issues? If we can't just wait and let our kids figure it out in their own timing, and we can't just tell them the way it is and leave it at that, then we need to find another way to get results.

Instead, speak truth with love and respect.

I'm going to be transparent here. I've spent a lot of my life studying the Bible. I get a huge charge out of discovering what I think are new and perhaps better ways to look at Scripture, and I've been known to engage people in a friendly debate now and then. *Ahem*. That passion was borne out of good intentions. I love God's Word, and I love digging into it deeply. That feeling of unearthing a nugget of truth hidden deep within the passages and nestled among the history and tradition is invigorating to me. But I've learned over the years that knowledge spewed without love just sounds hollow.

> **If I speak in the tongues of men or of angels**, but do not have love, I am only a resounding gong or a clanging cymbal. If I have the gift of prophecy **and can fathom all mysteries** and all knowledge, and if I have a faith that can move mountains, **but do not have love, I am nothing**. (1 Cor. 13:1–2)

The knowledge of the *content* of the Bible without a grasp on the intent—the love—and without giving it the proper *context*, will never reach our kids. I can speak to teens about ancient customs and the true meaning of a Greek word until I fall over. But if I don't lovingly apply it in a way that makes sense to them, to their own lives, I've done nothing more than sound like a clanging bell that rings in their heads until the last dong fades into nothingness. I can be right, but that doesn't mean I'll get through to them.

It's not as easy as just handing down the facts and expecting our kids to soak them up like sponges. It simply doesn't work that way. Teens can tell if you've really taken the Scriptures to heart and applied them to your own life, or if you're just trying to do your spiritual duty by passing the doctrine—the fire extinguisher—on to them. They can tell if you're preaching out of control and fear, or if you're reaching out to them out of love and concern. Make sure the Bible is a part of each and every discussion you have about the choices your teens will make. That way, they'll understand that you're passing along God's Word, rather than coming at them with a because-I-said-so attitude.

Here are a few questions to ask yourself:

> Have you prayed over the topic before bringing it up to your teen?
> Are you taking biblical ideals and making them relevant issues for a teen?
> Are you using too many personal examples or lectures?
> Do your teens feel free to ask questions? Are you prepared to give or find an answer if they do?
> Are you offering application techniques, or just handing down rules?

Proactive: Answering *How*

If we don't take the time to prayerfully pass down biblical truth and godly expectations in a modern way that appeals to our kids, then how can we fault them for not receiving it from us? Our babies come into the world fully trainable. We can't let go and expect them to teach themselves, because they will look for a source of education. It's your job to make sure you're the one providing it.

Instead, model by making right choices.

Here's the tough part, Mom and Dad. Do you live in such a way that you are above reproach? I speak to myself on this point as well. How can we ask our teenagers, who are far less prepared to deal with life's temptations than we are, to make good decisions if we're not modeling the right choices in front of them? How can we expect them to overlook our shortcomings and choose better for themselves? When things get tough, you'd better believe that they'll use our failures as an excuse to justify their own.

To offer the best life to your teen, you need to be living a righteous life yourself.

In 1 Corinthians 9, Paul writes to the church about this topic. He warns against preaching the truth to others but living in such a way that you miss it yourself:

> Therefore **I do not run like someone running aimlessly**; I do not fight like a boxer beating the air. No, I strike a blow to my body and make it my slave so that after I have preached to others, **I myself will not be disqualified** for the prize. (vv. 26–27)

Don't despair; this doesn't mean you have to be perfect. But you do need to be honest about your struggles and temptations. Let your teens know that living for Christ, defending truth, and standing up against sin aren't simple for you either. Relate to them with respect, and you'll get their respect back. Be open about the cost of doing the right thing so they'll know they're on the right path.

Imagine if, when you were a teen, your parent had responded to a problem you were having by saying to you, "You know what? I struggle with that too. It's not easy for me to make the righteous choice when it comes to _____ either. I do it because I know it's best for me and because I know God chose that as the way for me to walk, so I do my best to walk in it." How would this have made you feel? Would you have responded with the "dreaded eye roll"?

It helps teenagers when they can see their parents as human beings with weaknesses, failures, and struggles. They don't feel so alone in the struggle when they see the need we all have for the grace of God and the power of the Holy Spirit in battling sin.

Instead, provide "real life" practice.

Unfortunately, the best way young people learn is through personal experience. But we don't want to wait until they make the mistakes in order for them to learn from their mistakes. So, what can we do?

This is where these Hot Buttons books come in. When we use the Strategic Scenarios, purposeful dialogue about hot-button issues will provide us the opportunity to sneak in something resembling personal experience for our kids—without the dreaded ramifications—while also teaching them that their opinions and thoughts are important and valid.

CHECK POINTS

- ✓ Instead of trying to relate and be accepted by your teen as a contemporary, gain credibility by admitting and embracing your differences.

- ✓ Avoid communicating boredom or disinterest in your teen's life. If your teen feels like you just want her to go away, she will.

- ✓ Teens can tell if you have really taken the Scriptures to heart and applied them to your own life, or if you're just trying to do your spiritual duty by passing them on.

- ✓ Without giving it the proper *context*, knowledge of the *content* of the Bible will never reach our teens.

- ✓ If you don't apply it in a way that makes sense to them, to their own lives, you've done nothing more than sound like a clanging bell.

- ✓ To offer the best life to your teen, you need to be living a righteous life yourself.

- ✓ How can you ask your teen, who is far less prepared to deal with life's temptations than you are, to make good decisions if you're not modeling the right choices in front of them? How can you expect them to overlook your own shortcomings and choose better for themselves?

- ✓ Unfortunately, young people learn best through personal experience. This is where Strategic Scenarios come in.

PART TWO

Identifying the Internet HOT BUTTONS

When we were young, our sphere of youthful influence extended only as far as we could walk and still make it home before the streetlights came on. Even in junior high and early high school, we couldn't get to know someone outside of school unless we could ride our bikes to them or get dropped off at the mall to hang out. The telephone was our main communication tool, but parents limited our use because they needed the phone line free for other calls and they worried about high phone bills.

All that has changed. Most cell phone plans have unlimited texting, and astronomical or unlimited minute allowances. And the Internet has opened up manifold channels of communication. With webcams, blogs, and digital downloads, kids can chat endlessly online, share daily life stories, and exchange photos, all without ever leaving the house. In comparison with our meager sphere of influence, our teens today can have relationships that span the globe!

In these ever changing times, it's vital for parents to stay on top of the current trends and get there ahead of their teens whenever possible. By being prepared yourself, you'll best be able to get your tweens and teens ready to make good choices.

Internet
Activity

In the cyber world, there is always something new to do or some new distraction to take up time in nonproductive ways. In this fast-moving, graphics-driven society, our tech-savvy teens are drawn to flash websites and a vast array of social networks. Adolescents used to become enraptured by the television screen, but now it's the digital screen as they surf the Web for hours a day. Unlike television, the Internet is personal, portable, interactive, and connected to life—so it's far easier for our teens to form an addiction to it that will impede their social and educational development.

Over recent years, the Internet has evolved into a highly individual experience that elicits a high level of dependency on it. Who can function without email? What about photo storage or social connections? How many people remain completely unplugged from the cyber world? Very few.

Children are rapidly becoming digitally literate. In 2003, over two million American teens had their own website—with girls being more likely to have a website than boys (12.2 percent versus 8.6 percent).[1] They blog, share pictures, share music, talk about their lives. All of these seemingly harmless activities open our kids up for scrutiny and danger. And yet, too often, Mom and Dad don't even realize their kids know how to do those things.

The Internet is a good thing in many, many ways. But behind the seeming safety of the Internet curtain, bright, happy, and well-raised youth are suddenly willing to reveal startling personal information to complete strangers as though it means nothing and will go no further.

It was previously thought that unsuspecting teenagers were duped into opening up to strangers online by sexual predators who posed as teenagers. But recent studies have proven that most teens are aware that their new cyber friends are complete strangers often more than double their age (you'll read more about this in later chapters). Yet they continue on in the friendship, unaware of or blind to the real dangers they face.

Let's go over some facts:

> Twenty-seven percent of fourth to sixth graders are completely unsupervised when they go online.[2]

That's one-fourth of children ages ten to twelve who are allowed unsupervised access to the Internet (and the number increases for teens). *Whoa*. As this book continues through the online issues, you'll see how detrimental this can be to a child's safety and development. If your children are among those statistics, please consider changing your Internet use practices in your home. Immediately.

> Parents of children under eighteen who access the Internet estimate their children are online an average of *6* hours a week; however, children ages eight to twelve admit to spending an average of *11.4*

> hours online a week, and nearly a quarter report doing things online that their parents would not condone.[3]

My guess is that parents who say their kids are online an average of three hours a week are well-intentioned about their rules. They understand it's not healthy to grant unlimited access; they get that their children need boundaries. However, well-intentioned or not, they aren't following through with seeing that the rules are being followed.

> ➤ Only about three in ten young people say they have rules about how much time they can spend watching TV (28%) or playing video games (30%), and 36% say the same about using the computer. But when parents *do* set limits, children spend less time with media [TV, video games, computer]: those with *any* media rules consume nearly 3 hours less media per day (2:52) than those with no rules.[4]

It's clear that setting limits will benefit your kids. There are many suggestions throughout this book of specific boundaries you may decide to set. Prayerfully consider how your kids would benefit from being pulled away from the Internet and other forms of technology for more hours each day.

> ➤ Twenty-five percent of teens say their parents know "little" or "nothing" about what they do online.[5]

There is a lot of freedom represented in that statistic. Teens have hours and hours to hang out with a world full of strangers, and they have the impression that parents are clueless about what goes on online. It's no wonder the messes they're getting into.

> Compared to teens whose parents are less involved, teens whose parents discuss safe Internet practices with them are more concerned about the risks of sharing personal information and photos, and the risks of other online activities, and are far less likely to meet a stranger from the Internet in real life.[6]

This is where it's at, Mom and Dad. Parents who face the issues, who proactively press the hot buttons, are creating a safer environment for their kids. Internet safety involves a lot of factors and will require a lot of discussion. This book will help you do that and more.

Curiosity and the Cat

Aside from the social lifestyle of Internet usage, we also need to recognize that teenagers are curious about life. They want to know all of the secrets they believe are being hidden from them. It becomes their mission to find the answers and get one up on Mom and Dad. Human curiosity is perhaps at its peak during one's teenage years. In its basic, natural form, that curiosity is important for the maturing process. But, given the boundaryless World Wide Web, normal teen curiosity can lead to dangerous and detrimental situations and information, images, and experiences that will wreak havoc on that maturation process.

I must ask if you have a teen with unrestricted and private access to the Internet. If so, I implore you: please consider changing that immediately.

How can you protect your kids from something you can't see and don't know about?

Action Steps

It's absolutely vital that you not send a message to your teens that their Internet activity is private. If they feel private, they are far more likely to engage in inappropriate and extremely dangerous behaviors.

Whether in person or online, you have the right and the responsibility to know the whereabouts of your children and with whom they're communicating. Wouldn't you check up on where they're going on a Saturday night and with whom they're hanging out after school? Just the same, you should be monitoring the time they spend on the Internet, paying attention to what they do there and who they spend time with online.

> **Internet access in your home should be no more private than a conversation in a packed elevator.**

Yes, it will take more time and effort from you to monitor and stay on top of all the details. It will require more attention and more communication between you and your teens. I know you're busy; I know your teens will balk at added controls placed on them . . . but, honestly, I don't care. If just one of the parents reading this implements tighter restrictions on Internet usage and just one teen is saved from any number of dangers that we'll be talking about in upcoming chapters, then this whole book was worth it.

Letting children of any age access the Internet without supervision is like pushing them out of a plane without a parachute and expecting them to learn to fly on the way down.

The World Wide Web is an exciting frontier for teens—a world of freedom from the relative safety of their own homes, a world where they can be whomever they want to be and where they will find someone to appreciate them.

Or so they think.

Father, I'm sorry if I've dropped the ball and have been too permissive in the area of my child's access to the Internet. Help me pull back the reins and institute a safer structure. Please go before me and help my teens realize that I only have their safety and best interest at heart. As in every issue I face, when it comes to the safety and well-being of my children, please give me Your insight and wisdom. Help me see the truth of situations and know how to react. Give me peace and confidence to leave my kids in the safety of Your hands, knowing You're watching out for them. Amen.

CHECK POINTS ▶▶▶

GROVE FAMILY LIBRARY
101 RAGGED EDGE ROAD SOUTH
CHAMBERSBURG, PA 17202

CHECK POINTS

✓ Most teens are aware that their new cyber friends are complete strangers, often more than double their age, yet they continue on in the friendship, unaware of or blind to the real dangers they face.

✓ Internet activity in your home should be no more private than a conversation in a packed elevator, and shouldn't be treated as such.

✓ Whether in person or online, you have the right and the responsibility to know the whereabouts of your children and with whom they're communicating.

✓ Nearly one-fourth of children ages eight to twelve report doing things online that their parents would not condone.

✓ If you have a teen with unrestricted and private access to the Internet, please change that immediately. You can't protect your kids from something you can't see and don't know about.

Social
Networking

Ninety-six percent of students ages nine to seventeen who have access to the Internet have used social networking technologies.[7]

Facebook is the premiere social networking site for Internet users of all ages. Used correctly, it can be a great tool for relationship building, keeping in touch with friends, and sharing information among friends, both near and far. It can be a time waster, sure, but in general it *can* be harmless.

Twitter, Foursquare, LinkedIn, YouTube . . . these and similar sites are fine tools in the right hands, with appropriate boundaries and supervision. They are inherently neither good nor bad—it's all in how they're used. If you assume that nothing bad can happen on those sites, you're opening your family up to a world of danger. But access to these sites can be allowed in healthy ways that can actually benefit your teens.

> A long-term study conducted by psychologists at the University of Virginia assessed 172 youths at age 13 and 14 for qualities of friendship and popularity and then monitored their Internet use seven years

later. "We're finding that the interactions young adults are having on their Facebook and MySpace pages are more similar to than different from the interactions they have in their face-to-face relationships," said psychology professor Amori Yee Mikam.

Mikam's study found that those in the study who had positive face-to-face friendships were the same teens and young adults who used social networking sites to deepen and extend relationships. Youth in the study who lacked social skills and positive interactions in real life were more likely to use social networking sites in negative ways such as making threats, posting put-downs, and posting inappropriate photos of themselves.[8]

Other than those most commonly known social media sites, there are some others high atop the list of teens' favorites. You definitely need to know about these, and I would recommend you rush to your computer to see if they're accessible through whatever parental restrictions you have in place.

1. www.chatroulette.com

Chatroulette is a completely free website that facilitates random, unrestricted one-on-one webcam chats with strangers worldwide. When I went to the site to research, the first thing that popped up was a request for access to my camera and microphone. The focus is webcam communication, and there are no restrictions at all as to who can use the site.

So what's the problem? Anyone can log on at any time. This means that upon entry to chatroulette, your teen will be paired up for a conversation with anyone, anywhere, and have no control over the connection and what will be visible when the chat room opens—many times to a naked user or a camera focused on a user's genitals. *There are no age requirements or any other sort of block*, so your teen can log on anytime, and potentially be paired with, say, a pedophile from Australia who shows lewd acts on webcam the moment the chat opens. Even supposing your teen sensibly rushes right out of that chat, she will have seen things that are now burned in her memory. Forever.

2. www.formspring.me

Formspring is a pretty new site that seems to be best at perpetuating cyberbullying. Teens congregate on the site and leave negative, hurtful, and mean comments about each other. Someone asks a question and others answer. It can be as simple as "What kind of music are you listening to?" to something as potentially dangerous as "Do you think I'm pretty?"

So what's the problem? Most of the communication is negative. Almost nothing good comes out of this site, though fourteen million US citizens visit it monthly. This site is traumatic for many teens because it's a hotbed of hateful comments. It seems like people go there to take out their frustrations on others. According to a report by Trish Van Pilsum of Fox News, "The Q&A model is becoming a new social media trend, and there are other sites that follow the same format . . . but what makes Formspring different and enticing to bullies is that people can post anonymously."[9]

3. www.mylol.net

Mylol claims to be the number one site for teen dating and allows teens as young as thirteen to register. This quote from a thirteen-year-old was posted on the site mere minutes before I visited:

> *want a really flirtatious boy ;) 13 or 14 really nice no pervs!!*

I tried to imagine how I would feel if I saw that request next to a picture of my daughter. Once a member, teens can watch other users' personal videos, make friends with people from anywhere in minutes, use the "love tester," vote in photo competitions, and join live chats.

So what's the problem? The site is a gathering place for predators and contains thousands of adult users posing as teens, and just as many who are honest about their ages but pursue teens anyway.

4. www.hotornot.com

Hotornot.com allows users to rate others' photos and even meet the people whose photos are being rated. I have had personal experience with this site when someone submitted a picture of me for voting. I found out about it following a hacking incident when my Facebook account was taken over by a stranger. Even though I didn't look to see my ratings—what good could come of that?—I can definitely see how such an experience could destroy a teen's self-esteem.

So what's the problem? Rating sites are becoming more and more popular with teens because they're able to express their opinion with the click of a button. That level of anonymity makes teens feel comfortable saying things they'd never say in real life. The images they're rating don't seem real to them, and so they don't consider the potentially devastating outcome for the people being rated.

5. www.textsfromlastnight.com

TFLN is . . . oh boy, I don't even know how to describe this one. It's a place where people post the raunchy, ill-conceived, drunken texts they sent the night before so people can rip them to shreds for the stupid things they did or said, or praise the poster for a sexual conquest. Each text can even be ordered as a T-shirt.

So what's the problem? Beside the profanity, innuendo, blatant talk of sex acts, lewd advertising, and anything else you might list as inappropriate for teens? Oh, nothing.

This one about pushed me over the edge. Can you tell by the sarcasm? I often forget just how nasty people can be—even teenagers. And I was horrified to my core at how easy it was to access the nastiness because it's all right there on the front page with no filter at all. If we, as parents, don't do all we can to guard our teens from filth like this, it's no wonder they're so confused!

Warning Signs

In addition to closely monitoring what social media sites your kids visit, it is also important that you watch for evidence of social network addition.

How will you know if your child has moved from using social networking sites in appropriate ways to abusing them? These are warning signs you can look for:

- routinely loses track of time on these sites
- has less in-person, face time with people in favor of time on the computer
- shows anxiety if not near a computer
- stays up much later than his usual bedtime, perusing social networking sites without permission
- ignores favorite hobbies and previous interests
- forsakes important responsibilities like homework in favor of computer time
- thinks about social networking sites, even when she's not near a computer
- talks about online people as though they exist as a friend in real life

If your child exhibits some of these danger signs, you need to take notice and do something now, starting with a reevaluation of how much time and access your child has to the Internet. Next, consider what it is about the social networking sites that feed something important in your child, and seek other ways to meet that need.

There are some things you can do to help your child strike a healthy balance between real life and the cyber world.

Family time. Agree as a family to turn off the computer two evenings a week and hang out together. Maybe you can go outside the home one night and stay in one night. A third no-computer day could involve real-life friends outside the family.

First things first. Make a reward system where your kids earn computer time only after other responsibilities are accomplished.

Implement a time. Select a predetermined amount of time for computer use at a given time, then set a timer. When it goes off, the computer must be shut down. This helps make the limit objective, and you aren't the "bad guy."

Go unplugged. Consider an extended period of time to go unplugged as a family—a sort of "cyber fast," if you will. A week? A month? A summer? Do whatever you think will stretch the boundary enough to make an impact and affect some change.

Unplug Mon. through Thurs. Consider allowing no game systems, televisions, or recreational computer activity on school nights. With sports, youth group activities, music practice, homework, chores, and meals, there's not much time for anything else anyway, and this presents the opportunity for reading to make a comeback as a popular leisure-time activity.

Action Steps

Mom and Dad, you need to set rules and know how to enforce them. The cyber social world is a hotbed of danger for your teens, and if you plan to allow them access to it, you need know what's going on. If you're unclear about how to do certain things like check histories, filter websites, or receive reports, you need to educate yourself on those things, or pull the computer out of the house. It's vital.

Steps to take right away:

> Require your kids to provide you with log-in names and passwords to all of their networking accounts.

> Only allow your teens to use sites that provide a high level of privacy like Facebook, which has a setting to prevent non-friends from seeing any information or having any access.

> Prohibit the posting of pictures without permission. Your teens need you to enforce this rule. Remember, photos can be stored, altered, duplicated, and distributed, and 58 percent of teens don't think posting photos or other personal info on social networking sites is unsafe.[10]

> Help your teen understand the fact that teachers, coaches, recruiters, and professionals will look for information about students or applicants through online social media—this can affect job offers and college acceptance.

> Prohibit the posting of any personal information and making any purchases through online networking sites.

- If you find out there are secret networking accounts that weren't revealed to you, immediately suspend all computer privileges.
- Check up on your teens' activity frequently.
- Create your own accounts and "friend" your children at each site they frequent.
- Talk with your kids about what you see on the site.
- Require that they only "friend" people they know in real life.
- Require them to delete friends whose language and/or behavior is inappropriate.
- Check your children's chat histories and photo albums. (See chapter 9 for instructions on how to do this.)
- Have a zero tolerance policy for deleting histories—if it's gone, you know there was something to hide. (Chapter 9 explains how to check this.)
- Use parental control filtering software. (See the recommended resources at the end of this book.)

Many think that last suggestion is too extreme. They see it as a last resort and even then feel guilty implementing this strategy. I beg to differ with that line of thinking, and I've shared why in previous chapters. Parental control filtering software is one great way to protect your children as well as help you gather the information you need to keep them safe and smart on the Internet.

Is it a breach of your child's privacy to implement measures like these? Well, that depends on what you think is more important. Is it more important that you protect and keep watch over your maturing children, or is it more important that they have unfettered access to the globe—and the world have unfettered access to them?

Computer use is not a basic human right . . .

. . . it's not even something you have to allow in your home. It's perfectly fine (and not at all a breach of privacy) for you to make the deal with them that if they want Internet access, then you'll monitor it. It's as simple—and as wise—as that.

A top-quality software package works with social media sites to enable blocking of a specified site completely, or to implement all sorts of different restrictions or monitoring options. Some of the things you should look for when selecting the software that's best for you are:

- Customizability
- Ease of installation
- User friendliness
- Effectiveness of filtering

Top Ten Reviews rated the available parental control programs, and Net Nanny came out as the number one option.[11] Check out the recommended resource section at the end of this book for information on reviews of other software.

As you dive in and do the work it's going to take to keep your kids' hearts, minds, and bodies safe from potential findings on the Internet, you need to also take measures to protect yourself. Trust me when I say that even while researching for this book, I stumbled upon things I wish I'd never seen. Those visuals can't be erased from my mind, but I can pray the Holy Spirit would protect my heart from them.

I strongly encourage that, along with some of the software resources and other things I've mentioned within this book, you seek continued and updated information about the trappings of the net from reputable Christian sources like Focus on the Family. They do a fabulous job of providing parent tips, resources, and encouragement when it comes to raising tech-savvy kids in a Christian home.

Sometimes I feel so inadequate, Lord. How can I really be the parent You want me to be and protect my kids from all that's out there? This world is messed up and I need You to help me serve as Your emissary as I try to do the best I can. Show me what I need to see, Lord. Guide me to the trouble spots in my home, in my computer. Please help me help my kids. I trust You and I know You have them in the palm of Your hands. Please protect them from the enemy who wants to destroy them. Amen.

CHECK POINTS ▶▶▶

CHECK POINTS

✓ Access to social networking and similar sites can be allowed in healthy ways that can actually benefit your teens. Most are inherently neither good nor bad; it's all in how they're used.

✓ Certain sites pose a clear danger and should be banned.

✓ Make a plan about how to control the type and amount of plugged-in time your family allows.

✓ Substitute the hours you regain by reducing Internet time with activities that unite your family and encourage your faith.

✓ Parental control filtering software is a great way to protect your children as well as help you gather the information you need to keep them safe and smart on the Internet.

✓ Seek continued and updated information about the trappings of the net from reputable Christian sources like Focus on the Family.

Before we get into the truths about illegal file sharing, I want to point out that there are some legitimate ways to access material online for free. For example, free books can be found through Google books, Project Gutenberg, and online libraries. Pandora allows users to design their own channels for streaming their favorite tunes, and Noise Trade gives away music in exchange for social media buzz. Some television shows and movies are available through Hulu.com.

But even with the free offerings at their fingertips, teens are growing accustomed to accessing, downloading, and sharing digital content like songs, movies, and books without paying for them—otherwise known as *stealing*—the very instant they decide they want them. This has become such a common thing that many teens are desensitized to the criminal nature of these behaviors.

This makes sense when you realize there are over one hundred easily accessed p2p (peer-to-peer) programs available that anyone at all can download and install on a computer. These p2p programs make file sharing as easy as pressing a button. With such easy access, it's easy to forget that—depending on what file you share—

it's against the law. It feels very different than, say, walking into a store and pocketing a CD.

Let's look at some facts:

> When 10,000 seventh, eighth, and ninth graders were asked to describe what they use the Internet for, 22 percent said they commonly downloaded music they didn't pay for.[12] When teens are asked for their thoughts on the subject of whether file sharing is right or wrong, much of the debate centers around the idea that the music and movie companies have "enough money" and they should back off and let teenagers get the content they desire for free. Since when is that how our society functions? Some governments work their nation's economy that way, but not in a rogue, citizens-take-what-you-can manner.

> Kids as young as fourth grade have been caught pirating music, movies, and software online, and by the time they reach middle school, youth as a group engage in all known forms of cyber theft.[13]

Warning Signs

It's time to open your eyes and take a look around. Where did all that music come from? Where did the cache of movies come from? Someone expected to get paid for those things when they wrote, directed, produced, and marketed them, and you know how much money your teens have access to—so do the math.

Also, be aware, if illegal downloading is going on in your home, you share in the legal liability.

Which brings us to another point. Are you modeling scrupulous legal and moral behavior in regard to downloads and file sharing? Honestly, if your teens observe you snatching some music here and there or a movie now and then, this whole discussion is moot. You can't possibly expect to instill a strong moral code in your teens—one that guides them to do what's right even if they think no one is looking—if you're not living that way yourself. In fact, if you're doing it yourself, you should count that as a huge indicator that your teens probably are as well.

There's another important point aside from the legal issues: with downloaded music or movies, any sort of rating system becomes a non-issue. There's no way to set controls to regulate what your child is listening to or limit which files they are obtaining through those illegal methods. By the very nature of it having been stolen, it has slipped past the barriers of parental control. With that in mind, it's far better to get ahead of the piracy issue by instilling safe and healthy practices for Internet use in your home, training your kids to live within boundaries, and then staying on guard, keeping watch over Internet usage. And be sure you don't overlook handheld devices like iPods, phones, and gaming devices.

You can find peer-to-peer (p2p) file-sharing websites by searching your Internet history and watching the download history. Napster used to be one of the most popular p2p sites for sharing music until it was shut down by the US Justice Department. New sites pop up all the time, but some favorites include Limewire, Gnutella, Morpheus, and Kazaa. Keep an eye out for traffic going to those sites, but be aware that these aren't the only ones; new options become available regularly.

Action Steps

> Ill-gotten gains do not profit, but **righteousness delivers** from death. (Prov. 10:2 NASB)

The desensitization toward the illegality of file sharing has gotten to an extreme in our culture. I have two examples of this for you. The first one involves a student I know. He attended a laptop school—each student was issued a MacBook upon registration and it was on that computer that they did all their work, read their textbooks, and turned in their assignments. It's also where the entire student body passed around music and movies in a massive file-sharing explosion supported by some of the teachers.

I learned after this student graduated that the involved teachers would share movies and music with the students like there was nothing wrong with it. I just couldn't believe that professional adults would condone and perpetuate that kind of behavior. Public theft was being done in school, on school computers, involving students—the level of irresponsibility and immorality of that decision is unfathomable to me.

Another example involves a church worship director I follow on Facebook. For weeks I watched as he posted of his conquests—the movies he obtained for free. I was literally just about to confront him when the postings stopped. Someone must have beaten me to it. Did he not know what he was doing, or did he not care?

Has our society gone so far to the extreme that we can't even depend on our teachers and pastors to lead our youth to a moral high ground? Apparently.

So, Mom and Dad, it's up to you. Think about it. How would you react if you found your teen with a hundred CDs stolen from Target? Most parents would be horrified at such a finding, but many would think nothing of their kid downloading hundreds of songs without paying a cent.

Steps to take right away:

> Talk about file sharing and ask your teen to explain what it is just to see if he/she knows the truth of its illegality.
> Ask if your teen has participated.
> Make sure they are absolutely clear about three things: property equals ownership, copyright laws exist for a reason, and theft of copyrighted property is criminal.
> Work together to clean the computers in your home of any illegally obtained material. (Check MP3 players too.)
> Set up a system whereby your teen can do tasks to earn iTunes credits or some other way to acquire music.
> Look into Pandora.com—a great way to listen to music free on fully customizable, personal stations, and Noise Trade, which gives away music in exchange for social media buzz.

Mom and Dad, you need to teach your teens that they aren't owed anything frivolous like music or movies. Having tons of music in their player is not a basic human right, nor is it up to them to decide who has enough money or when it's okay to steal from them. Stealing is never okay.

> **You know the commandments**: "Do not commit adultery," "Do not murder," "Do not steal," "Do not bear false witness," "Do not defraud," "Honor your father and your mother." (Mark 10:19 NKJV)

It's so scary, Lord. How You must ache to watch the risky things we do with our lives and the blindness we have as parents. Now that I'm truly aware, I vow to be on top of this issue, Lord. I'll do the best I can, but I need Your help. Please show me the dangers that exist around my kids. Help me protect them and give them the insight to understand why I'm so concerned. I pray for my children and all of the children of this world who are potential victims for evil. I pray victory over the devil and willingness in my children to do the right thing. Please guide me and give me confidence to be the best watchman I can be. Amen.

CHECK POINTS ➤➤➤

CHECK POINTS

✓ Teens are growing accustomed to accessing, downloading, and sharing digital content like songs, movies, and books without paying for them—in other words, *stealing*.

✓ With such easy access, it's easy to forget that copyrighted file sharing is against the law. It feels very different than, say, walking into a store and pocketing a CD.

✓ If illegal downloading is going on in your home, you share in the legal liability.

✓ Take steps right away to determine what your teen knows about file sharing, and correct any faulty thinking.

✓ Remove illegally obtained materials from your family's devices, and make a way for your kids to acquire music and movies legally.

Internet
Porn

An adolescent's exposure to pornography is no longer limited to flipping through magazines he might find in a box hidden in the garage or the attic. No longer does he rush to the drugstore on the release day of the *Sport Illustrated* swimsuit edition. And she doesn't have to hide a ragged copy of a smutty book among the pages of her textbook to sneak peeks when no one is looking.

Those days are long gone.

"I watch it at home."
"Hard-core is my preference."
"It's as easy as turning on the television."
"It's all I think about all day, and I just can't wait to get home and alone in my room."

Sadly, those are actual quotes from teens when asked about their pornographic activity. Now, every teen is potentially faced with pornographic images on a daily basis, and some are bombarded with them hourly even if they have no desire to be. Clicking the wrong link, opening the wrong email address, typing the wrong phrase into a search engine. Unless you're closely monitoring all of your teen's online activities, they have most likely already seen graphic sexual images and the portrayal of behaviors they might not even understand.

Let's look at some facts:

> Forty-two percent of Internet users aged 10 to 17 surveyed said they had seen online pornography in a recent twelve-month span. Of those, 66 percent said they did not want to view the images and had not sought them out.[14]

> A whopping 80 percent of 15- to 17-year-olds are reported as having had multiple exposures to hard-core pornography.[15]

It's no surprise to most of us that porn is just a mouse click away—we've all stumbled upon it unwittingly. But it might be a surprise when you find out your teens are seeing and pursuing those images on purpose.

> CyberSentinel reported that the average teen spends 1 hour and 40 minutes each week surfing the Web for pornography.[16]

The Lie of Pornography

Pornography perpetuates lies that society often reinforces. The titillating ideal of pornography is to violate the nice girl, the pure girl. Viewing these fantasies that include rape, girls being drugged, orgies, and more, on a regular basis, has perpetuated a violent bent toward sex. Boys think that even the nice girls want "rough play," which often goes as far as rape. Girls think it's what they're supposed to do to get boys to like them . . . and so the cycle goes.

Teens are vulnerable to ideas about what the opposite gender and society expect of them. Viewing teen girls in pornographic films and seeing boys' reactions sends girls the message that this is what they need to do to compete in today's meat market. For boys, there is a subtle message that as soon as a boy reaches puberty, he should be viewing pornography and then living out its graphic scenes.

Another huge problem is that pornography never mentions things like teen pregnancy, STDs, AIDS, broken hearts, or regret. It's all a big party with no ramifications—at least that's the way it appears. Your teen will never stumble upon a scene where a girl tells a boy she's HIV positive; it's as though concerns like that don't exist. As the fantasy world of pornography becomes real in the minds of teens, those real-life concerns become a nonissue just as they are on the screen.

The dangers of viewing pornography:
- Objectifies women
- Justifies male stereotypes
- Encourages violence
- Creates addictions and cravings for more, more, more
- Leads to promiscuity, which leads to STDs and unplanned pregnancies
- Forms unrealistic expectations to which real-life relationships can never measure up
- Entices the viewer to lust, which can lead to masturbation (For more on this issue, see *Hot Buttons Sexuality Edition*.)

Smile for the Camera

With the addition of the webcam, participating in teen porn is as easy as pressing a button. Most laptops have a built-in camera, so making a video and emailing it or uploading it to a website is simple and integrated with many social networking sites like Facebook and Twitter.

Often, image sharing starts innocently—goofy pictures, funny faces, silly videos. Then it becomes more risqué as time goes on, and it takes on the tone of a dare leading up to the trading of sexually explicit photos, chats, and videos. Once it gets to that point, it's too late. Those pictures and videos are public and can follow that unknowing teen forever.

> Why would kids take this kind of risk? "Teenagers are not exactly known for their great judgment," notes Lawrence Balter, a professor of applied psychology at New York University. "They are sexual beings, of course, and they want to push the envelope. They're playacting. And they're impulsive. Generally, there's not a lot of thought before hitting the send button."[17]

They feel anonymous and safe in the privacy of their own home or their own room. That sense of privacy emboldens them to do things they wouldn't ordinarily do, without realizing that they're opening themselves up to a much more public issue than they ever thought.

Also, were you aware that a minor can be *guilty* of child pornography and prosecuted to the fullest extent of the law for possessing it? I almost want to repeat that just to make sure you don't miss it.

If your teen has sexually explicit pictures of another minor, that is punishable child pornography.

The penalties vary by state, of course. Findlaw.com has an interactive map that will allow you to see the laws in your area. (See recommended resources for more information.)

In April 2010, the *Tampa Bay Times* reported that Patrick Melton, age seventeen, became a sex offender after pleading guilty to fifty counts of possession of child pornography. The kicker? Many of the pictures and videos in his possession were people near his own age. Also interesting to note about Patrick: he stumbled onto porn when searching for "hot rods" on the Internet at nine years of age. He accidentally typed "hot bods" and has battled with pornography ever since, and now faces a lifetime of wearing the label *sex offender.*[18]

Consider how the lives of Patrick Melton and countless other teens who have been exposed to porn and its addictive nature might have been different with a little bit of restriction, some careful monitoring, and a lot of education.

Myths About Pornography

Myth: Nothing in the Bible specifically says that people shouldn't look at other naked people via computer, movie, or magazine.

Truth: People like to offer a "The Bible doesn't say . . ." excuse in regard to a lot of activities, and while it may be true to the letter, it's not true to the nature of God's will. Similarly, your teen may try to argue that God made the human body beautiful, and He created us as sexual beings, and by doing that He was saying it was okay to pursue sex and sexual images, especially since He didn't come right out and say "pornography is bad."

The fact is, God did outline His plan for us to have healthy sexual relationships within marriage, under covenant with Him; and viewing pornography, even as a teen, has lasting implications that can follow into marriage.

God had a very distinct plan for sexuality:

> Marriage should be honored by all, and **the marriage bed kept pure**, for God will judge the adulterer and all the sexually immoral. (Heb. 13:4)

Myth: Pornography is only wrong if there is a physical sex act. Viewing pornography isn't physical, and has no real connection with the subject, therefore it's not a sin and no one is hurt.

Truth: That is nothing more than another way to rationalize sinful behavior. Yes, people are hurt—both individuals and entire families—in the making and viewing of porn. Plus, Jesus made it very clear that sin is more than an act—it can be nothing more than a thought.

> But I tell you **that anyone who looks on a woman lustfully** has already committed **adultery with her in his heart**. (Matt. 5:28)

Myth: What I do in the privacy of my own home, my own room, is my own business.

Truth: As a parent, you can enforce rules and require obedience. But on this issue, as with most others, it's even better if your teens commit to purity for themselves. If they've chosen to keep themselves free of depravity, they'll be far better off and more likely to stick to their commitment than if they're just following your rules.

They need to declare for themselves:

> I will set **nothing wicked** before my eyes. (Ps. 101:3 NKJV)

> For God will bring every deed into judgment, including **every hidden thing**, whether it is good or evil. (Eccl. 12:14)

Warning Signs

What to watch out for:

> Your teen flips off the monitor or changes the screen when you enter the room
> Excessive amounts of time online—like it's difficult for them to pull themselves away
> The use of chat rooms and instant messaging
> Locked doors while the computer is in use
> Lies about the amount or type of computer use
> Withdrawal from family activities, sadness, overwhelming attachment to the cyber world
> Unhealthy outlook on the opposite sex
> Pornography on his/her computer. If your child says she/he has no idea how it got there, check the history of sites visited. You'll either find the log or it will be erased, either of which is a red flag.

Action Steps

It all seems so futile at times—believe me, I know. But, trust me, Mom and Dad, the battle you fight for your kids' safety, purity, and well-being is one worth fighting. The most important thing, and the reason for the Hot Buttons series, is to address these things proactively, not reactively.

Don't wait until your daughter's naked images are already serving as wallpaper on a malicious ex-boyfriend's laptop or posted on hotornot.com. Don't wait until you find out she knows how to use a webcam for all the wrong reasons. And please don't wait until you find out your son has been objectifying women and then treating his own girlfriend badly. Act now.

The hot button of pornography is an uncomfortable topic, but your tweens and teens need to hear about this from you before their friends sneak it into their lives. If you present it in the right way, you have a chance of creating a sense of horror about pornography—a right understanding of its dangers and evils—that simply won't be there if their friends introduce it to them.

Start talking about this *now*. Avoid just making rules—you want your teen to be your ally in the battle against pornography. Focus the conversation on their thoughts about it, and use words that will make an impact:

Ask point-blank if your son or daughter knows of kids who do these kinds of things. Ask how he or she would feel about seeing pictures or videos of friends . . . or even a sibling.

Use questions like:
> - What do you think of this?
> - How does that make you feel?
> - How do you think the person in the picture or video feels?
> - What does the word *objectified* mean to you?
> - What if it were your sister or your mother in that video?
> - What do you think some of the long-term risks would be with having pictures like that on the web?

Ask your kid for ideas to guard against that kind of exposure for themselves and even for their friends. Guide the discussion to talks of greater privacy controls, sharing less information on Facebook and other social media sites, and just saying no.

If your kids are embarrassed to have this conversation, be grateful that they aren't so desensitized that it doesn't even affect them. But don't let that embarrassment cause you to back down, thinking they aren't ready. The more you persist in making this a real issue that's out on the table, the less privacy and secrecy your teen will feel while on the Internet. Keep the dialogue open—one talk won't cover this issue forever.

Steps to take right away:
> - Set firm limits and be sure your teens know why your values are important to you on this subject.

- If you find the computer's web surfing history is often erased, do an impromptu check after your teen has been online for a while—before he or she logs off, when the history would likely be deleted.
- Emphasize the very real trouble teens can get into by sending or even just having pornographic photos or videos. It's not just against your home rules—it's a crime.
- Work through Strategic Scenarios 5, 8, and 13 in chapter 11 and come up with more of your own.
- Pray together.

> Finally, brothers and sisters, **whatever is true**, whatever is **noble**, whatever is **right**, whatever is **pure**, whatever is lovely, whatever is **admirable**—if anything is excellent or praiseworthy—**think about such things**. Whatever you have learned or received or heard from me, or seen in me—put it into practice. And the God of peace will be with you. (Phil. 4:8–9)

Father, I can't be with my children every moment. I can only do my best to keep them shielded from things, and to arm them with a readiness to run from evil. I'm comforted to know that You're with them at all times. Please look over their shoulders, convict them to turn the channel, to not click the link, to say no to peer pressure. Help them value the purity of their bodies and minds and to respect the purity of others. Call to their remembrance the values we've tried to instill. Amen.

CHECK POINTS ➤➤➤

CHECK POINTS

✓ Almost half of tween and teen Internet users have seen online pornography within the last twelve months. This is not a subject you can ignore.

✓ Pornography needs to be confronted proactively. Please don't wait until you discover it.

✓ The webcam has made teen porn as easy as pressing a button. Most laptops have a built-in camera, so making a video and emailing it or uploading it to a website is simple.

✓ Teens are vulnerable to ideas about what the opposite gender and society expect of them. Pornography plants the idea that even nice girls want "rough play," which often leads to rape.

✓ If you find your teen's web surfing history is often erased, do an impromptu check after he or she has been online for a while.

✓ Emphasize the very real trouble teens can get into by sending or even just having pornographic photos or videos. It's not just against your home rules—it's a crime.

If you were picking your child up from school one day and noticed a fifty-year-old stranger in the bushes snapping pictures of her as she walked by, what would you do? You'd become incensed, right? You'd involve the police and demand something be done. In the days and weeks following that incident, you'd probably start walking her to the fence around the school yard and waiting until she was safely inside. You would take every precaution you could, at least until you knew for sure the creep was locked up, right?

These days, a predator needs nothing more than a computer to gain access into a child's life. There is no protective fence and no surveillance in place to keep him out, other than your own vigilance and precautions. Recent studies show that one in seven youngsters has experienced unwanted sexual solicitations online, and one in three has been exposed to unwanted sexual material online.[19]

We've all seen the sting-operation television shows. We watch in complete fascination as forty-year-old doctors or pastors or teachers show up to have sex with thirteen-year-old girls. But in case you're unaware of the types of Internet activity that lead up to these liaisons, take a look at the following small portion of a real chat log used by Perverted Justice for *Dateline* NBC's To Catch a Predator series:[20]

> talldreamy_doc: hi how are you
> crazy_frazy2005: fabu. u?
> crazy_frazy2005: ur a dr?
> talldreamy_doc: yeah
> crazy_frazy2005: kewl
> crazy_frazy2005: what kind?
> talldreamy_doc: adults
> crazy_frazy2005: like ... old people?
> talldreamy_doc: yeah
> crazy_frazy2005: i love old people
> talldreamy_doc: thats nice
> talldreamy_doc: where do you live?
> crazy_frazy2005: near lakeville. u?
> talldreamy_doc: san Francisco
> talldreamy_doc: you have a picture ... i can share mine

This man, *talldreamy_doc*, is Maurice Wolin, age forty-nine. He was a doctor, but is now a convicted sex offender after this chat took a very steamy turn and he pursued this girl to the point of going to her house for the purpose of having sex with her. Thankfully, this was part of a sting operation and Maurice was taken off cyberspace before he managed to carry out his plans with this girl or any other young lady—maybe your teen.

If you or your kids think that nothing can happen to them online, that it only happens to others, or that adults exaggerate . . . think again!

A twenty-two-year-old registered sex offender now faces statutory rape charges involving a thirteen-year-old girl whom authorities say he met through Facebook. The Rowan County Sheriff's Office has charged Steven Lee Odom with three counts of statutory rape/sex offense and soliciting a child by computer, all felony counts.[21]

Not convinced? How about this one:

> NEW HAVEN, Conn. — Two men are accused in the sexual assault of two teen girls they met on a popular social networking Web site. Juan Carlos Coello, 19, of East Haven, and Julio Gambana, 18, of Brooklyn, N.Y., are accused in the sexual assault of two girls they met on MySpace.com. . . . Investigators said the men took the girls to a friend's home and sexually assaulted them at knifepoint. The assault lasted for a few hours into Sunday morning, according to police.[22]

A new study by Crimes Against Children Research Center finds dramatic growth nationwide in arrests of online predators who solicited law enforcement investigators posing online as juveniles—the numbers nearly quintupling from 644 in 2000 to 3,100 in 2006. Law enforcement officials estimate that as many as 50,000 sexual predators are online at any given moment.[23]

What makes that much worse is that 75 percent of the children studied were willing to share personal information with strangers in an online setting.

They feel safe online—which means we as parents and as a society have not done our job communicating the dangers present on the Internet.

The problem is that so many of our children are bored. They're home alone in the hours between the end of the school day and when Mom and Dad get home from work. They feel safe in their homes and anonymous on the Internet. They have no idea that there is a 50 percent chance that the stranger they're talking to in the chat room is a predator with malicious intentions toward them.

Tell me, could you be absolutely certain that your teen, without any preparation or understanding of how predators work, wouldn't have gotten sucked into that conversation with *talldreamy_doc* too? Bored, home alone after school, feeling safe in the confines of her own home. Remember, *one in seven* youngsters has experienced unwanted sexual solicitations online, and *one in three* has been exposed to unwanted sexual material online.[24] So, please believe that it's possible—even probable—without proper preparation.

How It Works

A predator lurks in the shadows of the places where he is most likely to find his prey. He's stealthy and patient, wise about when to hang back and when to strike. He knows from experience that he'll soon catch his next unsuspecting, unsupervised victim and it will be worth the wait.

Typically, a predator—often a middle-class family man—waits in chat rooms and online sites frequented by teens. They might hang out quietly in the background for a while, watching as the teenagers talk among themselves, tucking information aside to be used later. Maybe one afternoon, a teenage girl happens into the chat room before her other friends arrive, or stays late after they've left. He can then use some of the info he gleaned from previous conversations to strike up a friendly conversation with her.

In one scenario he might pose as a teenage boy and tell her that his legs are sore from cross-country practice.

She perks up. "I run cross country!"

"U do?" he asks innocently.

The rest is history. Eventually, he convinces her to meet him in person where she is raped and kidnapped . . . or worse.

That scenario shocks us, and yet we can understand how our teen could accidentally get mixed up in a tough situation under those circumstances and be completely victimized. But . . .

Would it surprise you to know that most teenage victims are approached by adults who admit their age?

Most Internet predators don't pose as teens to lure unsuspecting young girls and boys to a meeting site where they kidnap them. In fact, the American Psychological Association found that offenders pretended to be teenagers in only 5 percent of the crimes studied by researchers.[25]

Predators enter chat rooms, approach via email, meet up on gaming sites, and so on. Those adults hold back and let the teenager think she or he is driving the conversation. They steer and manipulate that teen into believing that this adult is special, loving, and looking out for a new online friend. They take time to develop and nurture the trust and confidence of the victims, who become dependent on these relationships that quickly become romantic love interests or sexual fantasies or adventures.

Why would teens want to subject themselves to that kind of experience? Often, teens are looking for acceptance, approval, love. They feel misunderstood at home. Perhaps have few friends. But sometimes it's a simple case of just wanting to see what it feels like. Our teens think they should have every experience that exists and are willing to take risks in this adrenaline-driven society to have those experiences. At any cost.

Take a look at the story of Pittsburgh thirteen-year-old Alicia Kozakiewicz. An average teenager by her own description, she, like most teens she knew, used the Internet to communicate with her friends and to make new ones. Eventually, she befriended an older man online who, through a chain of familiar circumstances, kidnapped her and kept her captive in a basement where she was tortured and sexually assaulted for four days.

Now, years after her horrifying experience, Kozakiewicz speaks to students all over the country, trying to get them to open their eyes to the evil realities that exist online. "This can really happen to them. We live in a world of denial. We see all these horror stories and these horror movies and they're movies. They're all entertainment. It's hard to differentiate between the two," Kozakiewicz said.

Sex Trafficking

Sex trafficking is a horror that only happens in Thailand and Cambodia, right?

Wrong.

There are at least 100,000 children prostituted in America every year and as many as 300,000, according to Shared Hope International, a Christian anti-trafficking organization.[26]

> "Men are buying younger children," Shared Hope founder and former congresswoman Linda Smith said. "They're buying more violent acts with the children, and those children aren't willingly saying 'I want to be prostituted.' Now we're seeing 9, 10, 11-year-olds. Eleven years old is common—snatched from a middle school, lured through a mall or online."[27]

There is no other period in human history when there have been more slaves—and never before has the slave trade been focused primarily on sex. Where we've made progress as a human culture in some ways, we continue to slip deeper and deeper into depravity when it comes to the issue of sex.

Usually, young girls are lured into connection with sex traffickers with promises of jobs, money, clothing, and modeling . . . and once they're in, they find they can't get out. Sometimes ever. Forced prostitution and pornography are the typical ways a teenage girl or boy may be used by sex traffickers. Traffickers force the minor to live in horrid conditions and suffer all sorts of abuse while having sex with strangers for money.

This is real. It's happening every day. And it's yet another reason to keep a tight grip on the Internet controls in your home. The Internet is a portal to the kinds of tragedy described above. When teens admit they freely speak with people they don't know on the Internet, when they share photos of themselves with their location metadata available, when they meet in person with "online friends," the nightmare of sex trafficking can easily become reality.

Warning Signs

There are plenty of signs to watch for that can alert you to the possibility that your child may be the target of an online predator.

- Long hours online
- Phone calls from people you've never heard of
- Gifts that arrive from strangers
- Excessive gifts, supposedly from friends
- Snapping off the computer in a rush
- Mood changes, defensiveness
- Change in sleep patterns
- Reluctance to discuss online activities
- Demanding more privacy, acting outraged when it's "violated"
- Deleted Internet history
- Sudden password changes
- Taking the laptop from room to room rather than just leaving it in one place
- Change in dress, diet, appearance

Internet Predators

- No time for friends
- Unexplained sleepiness—possibly due to late-night chats
- Has viewed pornography on the Internet and/or saved it onto the computer
- Uses the Internet at an external location like a local library or another person's home

Keep your eyes and ears open. Listen to your instincts. You can catch this early and prevent all sorts of tragic possibilities if you're alert.

Action Steps

I asked this of you in a previous chapter, but I need to drive this point home again. If any underage people in your home have unrestricted, private access to the Internet, I *implore you* to change that.

> **You might as well put up a billboard with your child's picture and say, "Here she is. This is her address. Come get her."**

And think about this carefully. Are there devices that access the Internet that you've forgotten about? Smartphones? Handheld video games? X-Box? Playstation? Gain control of anything and everything that links your teens to the cyber world.

Parents, you might not like me very much when I finish this paragraph, but I hope you'll understand my motives. If the computer or other Internet-connected devices have become a babysitter or a time waster for the teens and preteens in your home, then *you* are too busy or too distracted from your role as parent. You need to clear out some activities and responsibilities to spend more time with your kids. They should be at the bowling alley or the miniature golf course with *you*, instead of in a chat room being targeted by a predator. Time is all it takes: time for the hard discussions, time to hang out and play together, time to show what's most important in life.

The basic action steps for Internet usage in chapter 4 are foundational to protecting your kids, but it goes much deeper than even those restrictions. I urge you to take these additional action steps to protect your kids from Internet predators.

Steps to take right away:

> Make rules about what's allowed and what's not allowed, and then be prepared to enforce them.

> Talk to your child's school (or any place where kids could use a computer without your supervision) to find out if their Internet activity is monitored and to what extent. (What about when they spend the night at a friend's house?)

> Remind your child to never give out personal information such as a photo, their name, home address, school name, or telephone number online.

> Remind your child not to give out their email addresses as they often provide information about IP addresses (location), as do links and photos.

> Make sure phones and other devices are defaulted to not share location, which, along with times and dates, is often embedded in photos and shared on websites or through social media.[28]

> Be willing to stand up and say something if you witness unsafe behavior in other teens, and encourage your teens to do the same.

> Make your teen aware that there's a fifty-fifty chance that the stranger he's talking to is a predator. Are fifty-fifty chances good enough to take a risk?

You are my hiding place; **you will protect me** from trouble and surround me with songs of deliverance. (Ps. 32:7)

What If It's Too Late?

Do you think your child might have already talked to a predator? When it comes to the safety of your children, it's always better to be safe than sorry. If you have even the slightest feeling that they might have communicated with an Internet predator, you need to investigate.

◀ Forward any obscene or threatening messages you or your kids get directly to your Internet service provider.

◀ Contact your local law enforcement agency or the FBI if your child has received pornography via the Internet or has been the target of an online sex offender.

◀ Be sure to save and print emails written by a suspected predator.

- Check the caller ID on all the family phones and record any unidentifiable incoming phone numbers.
- Finally, you need to contact the police.

I'm not able to handle this one alone, Lord. The dangers that lurk behind the computer monitor are too dark for me to face alone. Please help me. Help me to be the parent I need to be, to make the time it's going to take to keep my family safe, and to be wise about all of the activities in my home. Help me to do the difficult things in the face of my teen's frustrations and confusion, and let any rules I implement be received well and honored. In the end, it's about the safety of my kids, Lord. So please protect them and use me in every way possible in the carrying out of that task. Amen.

CHECK POINTS ➤➤➤

CHECK POINTS

✓ Typically, a predator—often a middle-class family man— quietly lurks in chat rooms and online sites frequented by teens, watching as the teenagers talk among themselves, tucking information aside to be used later.

✓ Recent studies show that one in seven youngsters has experienced unwanted sexual solicitations online. One in three has been exposed to unwanted sexual material online.

✓ Law enforcement officials estimate that as many as 50,000 sexual predators are online at any given moment.

✓ Make your teen aware that there's a fifty-fifty chance that the stranger she's talking to is a predator—even if he says he's sixteen. It's not worth the risk.

PART THREE

Pressing the Internet HOT BUTTONS

We've discussed the dangers. We've looked at Scripture. We've addressed the probabilities of what your teens will face in the coming days, or what they've already encountered. We've considered the warning signs and recommended action steps to take—before it's too late. Now it's your turn. It's time to do the work. It's time to take a stand in your home and claim your teens' hearts and minds for the Lord.

I'm not talking about some sinister brainwashing tactic; I'm talking about training. It takes work to reach the hearts of teenagers and help them become conscientious servants of God who take ownership of their own choices and responsibility for all that passes in front of their eyes.

Protective
Procedures

It's that time in the process to start thinking about what you can do to make your home a refuge, safe from cyber intruders.

I'm going to list some possible rules and procedures you might want to establish in your family. We've talked about many of these already, but it's good for you to be able to see them all in one place

Also, this is a good time to remind you that Internet use refers to *any* online access—whether via computer, cell phone, video game, television, or handheld device. Be aware that many (if not most) newer cell phones and MP3 players can access the Internet. Make sure you implement these protective procedures for all devices that access the Internet.

And, Mom and Dad, I need you to partner with me on this. Commit to living above reproach on the issue of Internet use and pornography. If your teen walks in on you while you're looking at porn or finds some in your browser history, all the work you did to keep that teenager safe and healthy will be cast aside in favor of the implied permission they gleaned from your own behavior.

Basic Rules for Internet Use

- The Internet may only be accessed from public areas of the house.
- Don't open attachments without permission. Attachments can contain viruses that will invade your computer and open you to all sorts of risks.
- Don't click links. Links can subject your computer to a virus, but they can also lead you to places you don't want to go.
- Don't click on Internet pop-up ads because they might install spyware on your computer.
- Don't use passwords that people can guess like your pet's name, your birthday, or the name of your favorite sports team.
- Don't believe everything you read or see on the Internet because some of the information on the Internet is fake.
- Don't download pirated songs or movies or engage in any illegal file sharing.
- Don't delete browser history.

Social Networking and Chat Room Guidelines

- Limit use to one hour per day—better yet, three hours per week.
- All accounts and passwords must be immediately shared with Mom and/or Dad.
- Deleting Internet or chat history without parental permission is *forbidden*.
- Limit social media "friends" to real-life friends.

- Never accept a stranger into your network.
- Never post pictures anywhere online at all (or anywhere online without parental approval).
- Never give out personal information about yourself, your family, or your friends.
- Never agree to meet an online "friend" in real life.
- Never say anything online that you wouldn't feel comfortable saying in the same room as your parents.
- Choose a generic nickname not based on personal information (name, school, hometown), hobbies, or anything identifying.
- Never chat with a stranger—even with other friends present.
- Block strangers. Configure your IM program to block messages from anyone who is not on your contact/buddy list.
- Always report any questionable activity to your parents immediately.

Practices for Mom and Dad

1. Check online activity frequently. This is easy to do no matter what kind of computer you have. The instructions vary slightly depending on which Internet browser you use, so you should do an Internet search for instructions about how to view the Internet history in your particular browser. You'll be able to see the surfing habits of anyone who uses the computer. Regularly monitor the search habits and traffic patterns of your teens throughout the Web. Realize, though, that savvy teens will know how to delete some or all of their Internet history, so you want to keep an eye out for that too. Let your teen know that if the histories are ever erased, Internet access is suspended until further notice.

2. Check chat histories. If your teen uses a chat program like Yahoo Messenger or Skype, you can check the histories of these programs to see what the chat topics have been. Again, it's possible to delete these histories, so it's best to check often and watch out for large gaps of time with no conversation. Let your teen know that if the histories are ever erased, Internet access is over for a while.

3. Install filtering software to block undesirable Web content. Check out the recommended resources at the end of this book for information on how to find the software, or revisit chapter 5 to read a more in-depth discussion of the hows and whys of filtering software.

4. Use reporting software to let you know where your teens have been online and what they've been doing/saying. Most filtering software includes a reporting software in the package.

5. Follow through. Don't threaten without following through. If you tell your teens not to delete the chat history but then you never check on it, they may watch themselves for a while, but eventually let their guard down and get too comfortable with what they say and do.

6. Communicate. Communicate. Communicate. The key to all of these protective procedures is communication. Let your teens know what the rules are and why they're necessary. Communicate the consequences for broken rules. Talk about how they should handle things such as pop-up ads, links, or attachments.

The Armor
of God

As it pertains to hot-button issues like Internet activity, the "armor of God" is not simply a word picture in Scripture but a practical resource for navigating the spiritual battles Christ-followers face. Before you move forward to attack these Internet hot buttons in the next few chapters, I want to lead you through a symbolic application of the armor of God.

Below, you'll find a breakdown of Ephesians 6:10–17. Each phrase is followed by a bit of commentary and application, and a few directions. But please take note, there is nothing divinely prescribed in these specific directions. Perhaps there are other actions you can take that will hold greater meaning for you; in that case, feel free to improvise. However, please take this seriously. More than a silly exercise, this is a physical display of your faith in God's power and your acceptance of His protections.

Be strong in the Lord and in his mighty power. (Eph. 6:10)

A full measure of the strength and wisdom you need as a parent comes from God. His supply is sufficient to meet your needs, and you're not in this alone. You don't have to have eyes in the back of your head or some kind of supernatural insight into the cyber world—because He does.

Do this: Raise your open hands in surrender, ready to receive from God and expectant that He'll grant you strength, wisdom, and grace.

Pray this: *Father God, please help me to remember that I stand in Your might, not in my own. Let me rest in Your power and walk as a parent in Your strength. Guide my senses with Your knowledge and help me to know when I need to dig deeper into the Internet activities of my children or set tighter boundaries.*

Put on the full armor of God, so that you can take your stand against the devil's schemes. (Eph. 6:11)

The Lord is ready to uphold you as you face the enemy who seeks to harm your kids. The armor of God allows you to take your stand. There are many spiritual battles you'll have to face along the way. Sometimes you'll feel victorious and powerful sometimes you'll feel spent and weakened in your flesh. The armor of God is the promise that you can operate in His Spirit and His power. Though you may feel defeated at certain points on the path, you are assured ultimate victory when the process is complete in Christ. Do you remember our discussion of Philippians 1:6 from chapter 3? He started the work. He'll finish the work. It's a promise.

Do this: Stand strong. Confident. Like a soldier waiting for orders.

Pray this: *Prepare my body to receive Your armor. Place it carefully that I might be protected as a parent. Please protect my children and teens in the same manner that Your armor protects me. Guard their mind, body, and soul from the attacks of the enemy and give me the wisdom to teach Your truth. Help my kids see the power in Your mighty armor and give them the desire to claim it in their own lives. Guard their eyes, hands, mouths, and bodies. Help them run from danger and stand strong against temptation.*

> For **our struggle is not against flesh and blood**, but against the rulers, against the authorities, against the powers of this dark world and **against the spiritual forces of evil** in the heavenly realms. (Eph. 6:12)

You see, your real fight isn't against the predators, the peer pressure, or the temptations. Your battle is against your enemy and his dark forces.

Do this: Place your hands on a computer in your home.

Pray this: *Give me Your power over the evil in this world that seeks to destroy my family. Let me see clearly what's happening, what I need to know, and what I need to do—and then help me to do it!*

> Therefore put on **the full armor of God**, so that **when the day of evil comes**, you may be able to **stand your ground**, and after you have done everything, to stand. (Eph. 6:13)

With God's armor, you can face anything. Like a frontline soldier, you'll be prepared, protected, and powerful.

Do this: Close your eyes. Imagine you're a soldier on the front line of a battlefield, waiting to face the oncoming army.

Pray this: *I commit to remaining steadfast, unmovable, unrelenting in my battle against the dangers of the World Wide Web in my home.*

> Stand firm then, with **the belt of truth** buckled around your waist . . . (Eph. 6:14a)

During times of battle, the tunic was belted to secure the soldier's clothes and keep every part of the armor in place, allowing him to move more freely.

Do this: Buckle a proverbial belt around your waist. Then imagine that your kids are standing in front of you and go through the motions of putting a belt on each of them.

Pray this: *Let the belt of truth give us confidence and mobility to avoid our enemy's schemes.*

... with the **breastplate of righteousness** in place ... (Eph. 6:14b)

The breastplate protects the heart.

Do this: Symbolically, don the breastplate; then place it upon your kids. Your enemy wants you to feel silly, but resist that. This is a symbolic act that will mean something to you when you're finished.

Pray this: *Let Your righteousness, Lord, be a shield about this family. Be our protector and the lifter of our heads.*

... and with your feet **fitted with the readiness** that comes from **the gospel of peace**. (Eph. 6:15)

You're ready. You have the information you need and you're covered in prayer. Now it's time to get ready to go out and face your battle.

Do this: Lift each foot and plant it down hard.

Pray this: *I am confident in Your Word, Lord. I believe that You have led me and prepared me to be my children's very best advocate in this world. I am prepared to fight as Your ambassador, ready with Your Word.*

In addition to all this, take up **the shield of faith**, with which you can extinguish all the flaming arrows of the evil one. (Eph. 6:16)

Notice, the shield is active, not simply defensive. You're not merely blocking the enemy's arrows and sending them back out to do damage somewhere else; you're *extinguishing* them. Apply this truth about the shield of faith to the evil that lurks in the cyber world.

Do this: Raise your arm as though you hold a shield and wave it in front of you. Go to your computer and imagine your kids are sitting at it. Wave your shield around them and over your computer.

Pray this: *Put out the flaming arrows of evil in the cyber world, Lord. Let this shield of my faith swallow them whole, so that they would disappear, never to harm another soul again.*

Take the **helmet of salvation** ... (Eph. 6:17a)

The helmet protects your mind from doubt, fear, anger, carelessness, apathy, and other lies from your enemy.

Do this: Place the helmet of salvation securely over your head, to your shoulders. Imagine your kids are standing before you, and reach out to secure a helmet on each of them too.

Pray this: *I rest in my salvation, Lord. You are mighty to save and faithful to preserve.*

... and **the sword of the Spirit**, which is the word of God. (Eph. 6:17b)

You're armed and ready to fight. In the following chapters I will walk you through the next action steps in your battle for your family.

Do this: Raise your sword, which is the Bible—the Word of God.

Pray this: *I am equipped and ready to fight Satan's schemes against my family. I need You, Lord, to guide me and show me what my next move should be. Keep my heart and mind open to the truths and possibilities of what my kids face. And help them, Lord, to have the strength to say no, the wisdom to look away, and the passion to chase hard after You. Amen.*

Strategic
Scenarios

The first few chapters of this book identified why it's necessary to proactively press the hot buttons with your teens—and gave a few guidelines for when and how to do that. Part 2 outlined the specific hot buttons associated with the Internet, cyber safety, file sharing, and Internet predators. You have prayerfully put on the armor of God. Now it's time to affect real change and make a lasting impact in your home by using Strategic Scenarios with your teens.

Strategic Scenarios are pretty simple. You'll begin by telling your tween(s) and/or teen(s) a short story as though it's actually happening to them. You'll then present them with a few optional responses to the situation (don't give any indication of which response you think is better or worse). Allow them to choose the most natural personal response (without any judgment or comment from you). Once they make their choice, you will lead them through the discussion points and refer them back to relevant material you read earlier in this book. At the end of each discussion, you should give them the opportunity to change their original decision if they desire, and invite them to commit to wise choices in the future.

The important thing, when you begin this process, is to pray for guidance. You want to be open to the leading of the Holy Spirit so you can discern when to push an issue, and when to let it be. It's also important to approach the use of Strategic Scenarios carefully. You don't want to bombard your kids with topics all at once. Take it slowly and alternate between the various issues presented in the Hot Buttons book.

Also, you don't have to pretend you're making all this up as some big stroke of genius. It's okay to admit you're reading a book and this practice was suggested. After all, why not show your kids that you vigorously pursue new ways to reach and teach them? Trust me, once you begin, even if you're simply reading from the book at first, the conversation will develop; kids are desperate to work this stuff out.

In my family, these worked best around the dinner table. Sometimes we'd get through two or three over the course of a meal, but often just one would spark enough discussion and we wouldn't get any further. That's okay—in fact, that's wonderful. Communication is the goal, so don't stifle that in order to move on to the next scenario.

Some other places you might open Strategic Scenarios discussions are:

- in the car
- in a waiting room
- on a walk or bike ride
- while on a family date night

So, pretty much anywhere a conversation can take place!

If you have children of varying ages, don't shy away from doing these together. I'm a firm believer in getting the issues out on the table well in advance of the peer pressure. So, if your slightly younger children are going to be introduced to a concept relatively soon anyway, you'd much rather it come a bit sooner through these controlled and monitored means.

As you approach each topic, be careful not to preach. Allow your kids the freedom to work out the issue in this safe environment. Enjoy this process as it opens the lines of communication between you and your kids.

I won't lie, Mom and Dad, this is going to take work—lots of work. Are you ready for that? Are you convinced that you must put the time in with your teens and wage the battles now to help them win the war? The Internet is a very real and lasting part of our society. It isn't going away, and it can't be ignored. It's also not an issue your kids can figure out alone. Don't leave this one to chance, parents. Put in the time with Strategic Scenarios and reap the rewards.

Parents, tell your teen this story.

Like most afternoons, you're chatting with a bunch of school friends [if possible, use some names of your teen's friends] on a social networking site. After a few minutes, a new girl joins the conversation. Then another one. They blend right into the discussion and you find out that they were invited to the chat by one of your good friends.

You send him a private message: **How do u know these girls?**

He replies: **Met them on MySpace. They're cool.**

Uh oh. You realize immediately that he's never actually met them in person, what do you do?

Now offer the following options with no personal commentary.

Let your teen think about the choices and make an honest decision.

> A. You prod your friend for more info and tell him you're uncomfortable chatting with strangers—not to mention breaking rules—but you don't leave the chat just yet. After all, there's safety in numbers.
>
> B. You jump right into the conversation hoping to meet some cute new girls.
>
> C. You leave the chat immediately and recommend that your friend leave too. You stress the dangers of meeting strangers online.
>
> D. You leave the chat and tell your parents that some strangers have been conversing with you and your friends.

Crucial Step

Use this scenario as a jumping-off point for a discussion about chatting with strangers online. Be very careful not to sound judgmental or accusatory. Remember, your teen is exploring thoughts and first impressions—these aren't actual choices . . . yet. Parents, remember to keep your cool no matter how your kids respond; you want to make open discussion a natural part of your relationship with them, not a minefield they need to navigate.

Discussion Points

- Why did you make the choice you did?
- C is good but D is better. Why? (It's good to ignore the request but even better to involve an adult.)
- Communication is important. Adults can't protect you if they aren't made aware. Parents want to keep you safe, so involve them.
- Issues involving your safety, or that of others, require the help of an adult.
- A new "friend" may not actually be who he or she looks like in his or her picture.
- Share statistics from chapter 8.
- If you don't report the stranger, someone else might. But what if it's too late?
- Do you now have a different view on this scenario than you did at the start? Why or why not?
- Would you like to change your answer or stick with it?

Jesus said, "If you **hold to my teaching**, you are really my disciples. Then you will know the truth, and **the truth will set you free.**"

(John 8:31–32)

Parents, tell your teen this story.

You're really into music and would love a full MP3 player like all your friends have. The problem is, you just can't afford to buy the music, and your parents aren't willing to pay for much of it because they think free radio is good enough at your age. Your friends show you how to get music for free with simple downloads. They assure you that everyone does it—that it's how they all have so much music on their players. Since it's so easy and everyone else does it, it can't be all that bad, can it? You're so tempted—what do you do?

Now offer the following options with no personal commentary.

Let your teen think about the choices and make an honest decision.

> A. What would it hurt to try it once? You download two or three songs and promise to stop after that.
> B. You go for it. Why should everyone else have all that music except you? Besides, the music companies make too much money anyway.
> C. You politely decline and change the subject.
> D. You say no and then talk to your friend about stealing.

Crucial Step

Use this scenario to guide a discussion about file sharing and illegal downloading. Be very careful not to sound judgmental or accusatory. Remember, your teen is exploring thoughts and first impressions—these aren't actual choices . . . yet. And, if you need to confess and repent of your own wrongdoing in this area, Mom or Dad, this is a good time to come clean to your kids after you've repented (see part 4).

Discussion Points

- Why did you make the choice you did?
- Illegal downloading is stealing.
- It carries legal consequences.
- "Everyone does it" is just a rationalization to try to make a wrong right.
- No one is "owed" property that belongs to someone else, no matter how much money the others make.
- Discuss the statistics and points made in chapter 6.
- It's okay to tell a parent and let him or her handle it, but even better if you can confront the issue yourself and see if it gets resolved.
- Do you now have a different view on this scenario than you did at the start? Why or why not?
- Would you like to change your answer or stick with it?

The commandments, "You shall not commit adultery," "You shall not murder," "You shall not steal," "You shall not covet," and whatever other command there may be, are summed up in this one command: **"Love your neighbor as yourself."** Love does no harm to a neighbor. Therefore **love is the fulfillment** of the law.

(Rom. 13:9–10)

Strategic Scenario 3

Parents, tell your teen this story.

Just for fun, one of your friends posts a picture of you and several others on a site called hotornot.com where the pictures will be rated by strangers for their relative "hotness." Your parents don't let you go to sites like that, but you're dying to know what people are saying about you. What do you do?

Now offer the following options with no personal commentary.

Let your teen think about the choices and make an honest decision.

> A. No way would you go to that site—you want nothing to do with it, and you take it no further.
>
> B. You won't go there because your Internet history would show it, but you ask your friend to check it out and report back.
>
> C. How could you not go look? It's way too interesting to ignore, so you head right over there.
>
> D. You refuse to access the site, and you let your friend know that if she keeps going there, you'll have to let her parents know for her own emotional well-being.

Crucial Step

Use this scenario to guide a discussion about accessing harmful social networking sites. Be very careful not to sound judgmental or accusatory.

Remember, your teen is exploring thoughts and first impressions—these aren't actual choices . . . yet. Be prepared to stand strong on this issue, even if your teen minimizes it as harmless.

Discussion Points

- Why did you make the choice you did?
- People are mean, and they aren't even always honest in what they say, so what good could come of reading the comments?
- Asking your friend to access the comments and report them to you is putting her at risk.
- Share information from chapter 5. (Don't be afraid to discuss the actual sites mentioned in this chapter—let your teen see that you're informed.)
- Where did the friend get the picture of you in the first place?
- Which is better, A or D? A is great—but it's one-sided. It's important to share truth and wise living with others.
- Do you now have a different view on this scenario than you did at the start? Why or why not?
- Would you like to change your answer or stick with it?

> Hold on to
> what is good,
> **reject every**
> **kind of evil**.
> (1 Thess. 5:21–22)

Strategic Scenario 4

Parents, tell your teen this story.

Your parents never let you do the things your friends do. You're the only one of your friends who doesn't have a cell phone. You still have a bedtime. You still have to do chores. It's like they think you're nine years old! The worst part is that you're not allowed to be on the Internet for anything other than studying. No Facebook, no Twitter—no social media sites at all. But now that basketball season is over, you have quite a bit more time on your hands while Mom and Dad are at work. It's really tempting to set up a Facebook account and use it while you're supposed to be doing your homework.

What do you do?

Now offer the following options with no personal commentary.

Let your teen think about the choices and make an honest decision.

> A. You laugh off the temptation. While you'd like to do it, there's no way you'd disobey in such a blatant way.
>
> B. You don't do it, but you let your friends know that you're available for live phone calls during that time. At least you'll be able to keep up communications that way.
>
> C. Mom and Dad are way wrong on this one. Plain and simple. You go ahead and set up a Facebook account under a name they'll never figure out and promise yourself that you'll only friend a few people.
>
> D. You go all out. If you're going to do it, you might as well go big. Facebook. Twitter. MySpace. Whatever you can find—you create profiles, add pictures, and start chatting.

Crucial Step

Use this scenario to guide a discussion about social media. Be very careful not to sound judgmental or accusatory. Remember, your teen is exploring thoughts and first impressions—these aren't actual choices . . . yet. Parents, when your kids complain about house rules, honestly listen and respond to their specific concerns or requests rather than automatically saying no to every complaint they raise. If your motivation is truly their protection, they'll respect that, and even more so if you take their side sometimes.

Discussion Points

- Why did you make the choice you did?
- Do we obey only when we agree?
- Private accounts will only lead to danger.
- New "friends" may not actually be who their pictures portray.
- Review chapter 5.
- Maybe your parents won't find out, but what would happen if they did?
- Do you now have a different view on this scenario than you did at the start? Why or why not?
- Would you like to change your answer or stick with it?

Children, obey your parents in the Lord, for this is right. "**Honor your father and mother**"—which is the first commandment with a promise—"**so that it may go well with you** and that you may enjoy long life on the earth." (Eph. 6:1–3)

Strategic Scenario 5

Parents, tell your teen this story.

You're hanging out at your boyfriend's house and his parents aren't home—which is already a problem because that's against the rules. Then he takes out his laptop and clicks a link . . . a pornographic movie begins to play. He settles back on the sofa and waits for your reaction. What do you do?

Now offer the following options with no personal commentary.

Let your teen think about the choices and make an honest decision.

A. You ask him to turn it off right away—you don't want to watch that because it makes you uncomfortable.

B. You're afraid that if you say no, he'll think you're a prude. Just a few minutes won't hurt anything and no one will know.

C. You're horrified that he doesn't know you well enough or doesn't care about you enough to know that's inappropriate. You ask him to take you home. He's not the kind of boy you want to date.

D. Wow. You've heard about those movies, but have never actually seen one. You decide to watch it and see what the fuss is all about.

Crucial Step

Use this scenario to guide a discussion about pornography. Be very careful not to sound judgmental or accusatory. Remember, your teen is exploring thoughts and first impressions—these aren't actual choices . . . yet. Mom and Dad, if you don't already have a rule forbidding kids from being alone in the house with the opposite sex, make one! You can see here how easy it would be for a boyfriend (or girl-friend) to expose your teen to porn on the Internet.

Discussion Points

- Why did you make the choice you did?
- Your convictions are worth more than making a boy happy.
- A few minutes hurts a lot—you can't erase what you've seen.
- "I will set nothing wicked before my eyes" (Psalm 101:3 NKJV).
- Viewing these fantasies—which may include rape, drugs, and orgies—on a regular basis has perpetuated an unrealistic expectation of, and a violent bent toward, sex.
- Protect yourself by not spending time alone with a date.
- Chapter 7 has a lot of information on the topic of pornography. Refer to it as necessary.
- Do you now have a different view on this scenario than you did at the start? Why or why not?
- Would you like to change your answer or stick with it?

Finally, brothers and sisters, **whatever is true**, whatever is **noble**, whatever is right, whatever is **pure**, whatever is **lovely**, whatever is **admirable**—if anything is excellent or praiseworthy—**think about such things**. Whatever you have learned or received or heard from me, or seen in me—put it into practice. **And the God of peace will be with you**. (Phil. 4:8–9)

Parents, tell your teen this story.

You're at youth group and everyone is zapping each other songs from their laptops. You know they were downloaded through an illegal file-sharing program and now they're being passed around for free. Your youth leader offers to share with you too. You do love the music he's offering, and you haven't had the money to buy it on iTunes yet. What do you do?

Now offer the following options with no personal commentary.

Let your teen think about the choices and make an honest decision.

A. You jump at the chance. Everyone does it, and if your youth leader is doing it, it must be okay.

B. Politely decline and go do something else across the room so you don't have to think about what they're doing.

C. Decline and ask to speak privately with the youth leader. Let him know that you're disappointed to see illegal activities going on at youth group and ask him to consider praying about what he's doing and setting it right.

D. Tell a parent or pastor.

Crucial Step

Use this scenario as a jumping-off point for a discussion about file sharing and illegal downloading. Be very careful not to sound judgmental or accusatory. Remember, your teen is exploring thoughts and first impressions—these aren't actual choices . . . yet. Gray areas encourage your kids to break the law. Don't send the message that that's okay with you.

Discussion Points

- Why did you make the choice you did?
- File sharing is stealing.
- It carries legal consequences.
- "Everyone does it" is just a rationalization to try to make a wrong right.
- It's okay to tell a parent and let him or her handle it, but even better if you can confront the issue yourself and see if it gets resolved that way first.
- Parent: Do you have things you'd like to confess on this issue? (See part 4.) If so, make a commitment to your kids to live above reproach in regard to this from now on.
- Discuss chapter 6.
- Do you now have a different view on this scenario than you did at the start? Why or why not?
- Would you like to change your answer or stick with it?

Do not steal.

Do not lie.

Do not

deceive one

another.

(Lev. 19:11)

Parents, tell your teen this story.

You're supposed to be doing homework, but you have Facebook open while you do your research so you don't miss anything—after all, who doesn't? After catching up with a few friends who are online, supposedly working on the same project, you turn back to your work.

Bleep. A little box pops up and you're notified of a new Facebook friend request. You don't recognize the name, so you peer closer at the profile picture. It's a really cute boy about your age, but you've never seen him before. It says he lives nearby, and he sure looks nice—he has the straightest, whitest teeth you've ever seen. People say you can trust guys with good teeth. So, what do you do?

Now offer the following options with no personal commentary.

Let your teen think about the choices and make an honest decision.

> A. You eagerly turn your thoughts from your homework toward this adorable guy and accept his request. It's only online—not like you're meeting him in person. Plus, maybe he can help with your project.
>
> B. You ignore the request until your parents get home and ask one of them if it's okay to start a Facebook friendship with a stranger. In the meantime, you work on your project so you can be finished and maybe mess around on the computer all evening if your parents say it's okay.
>
> C. You delete his request without responding and tell no one because if you did, your parents would know you were doing more than just your homework. Surely the guy is harmless, but if he isn't, someone else will report him.
>
> D. You call the police.

Crucial Step

Use this scenario to guide a discussion about online safety. Be very careful not to sound judgmental or accusatory. Remember, your teen is exploring thoughts and first impressions—these aren't actual choices . . . yet. Mom and Dad, really think about how you want your teen to handle this situation before you launch into the scenario. There are several options—always err on the side of safety.

Discussion Points

- Why did you make the choice you did?
- C is good but B is better. Why?
- Talk about how it's good to ignore the request but even better to involve an adult.
- Communication is important. Adults can't protect if they aren't made aware. Parents want to keep you safe, so involve them.
- New "friends" may not be the person their pictures portray.
- Maybe someone else will report him, but what if it's too late?
- Calling the police is always an option if you feel at risk—like if you gave out your address before you wised up. But if you aren't in immediate danger, you should save all chat records and talk to your parents first.
- You can reread about social networking in chapter 5 and predators in chapter 8.
- Do you now have a different view on this scenario than you did at the start? Why or why not?
- Would you like to change your answer or stick with it?

There is **a way that appears to be right**, but in the end it **leads to death**. (Prov. 14:12)

Strategic Scenario 8

Parents, tell your teen this story.

You get an email message that appears to be from a friend of yours. There's a link inside the message that says it will take you to a YouTube video of a cat playing the piano. That sounds funny so you click the link, but it takes you to a website with pictures of naked people doing things you've never seen before. What do you do?

Now offer the following options with no personal commentary.

Let your teen think about the choices and make an honest decision.

A. You tell a parent right away.

B. You close the window immediately, but you don't say anything—you're too embarrassed. You then search for a way to delete the history so no one knows you visited that page.

C. You're fascinated with what you're seeing so you look around the website for a while and then bookmark the page for a later visit.

D. You don't want to get your friend in trouble so you don't tell anyone, but you reply that you'd prefer not to receive that stuff anymore.

Crucial Step

Use this scenario to begin a discussion about pornography. Be very careful not to sound judgmental or accusatory. Remember, your teen is exploring thoughts and first impressions—these aren't actual choices . . . yet. Parents, depending on how open you've been in the past, some discussions might be embarrassing, both for you and for them, but don't back away. It's too important, and it will get easier in time.

Discussion Points

- Why did you make the choice you did?
- Curiosity is normal, but those things are wrong.
- Don't follow links unless you know the website.
- The friend's email was likely hacked; you need to let his or her parents know.
- Once you see those images, you can't erase them from your memory.
- "I will set nothing wicked before my eyes" (Psalm 101:3 NKJV).
- Pornography is covered in detail in chapter 7.
- Do you now have a different view on this scenario than you did at the start? Why or why not?
- Would you like to change your answer or stick with it?

Finally, brothers and sisters, **whatever is true**, whatever is **noble**, whatever is **right**, whatever is **pure**, whatever is lovely, whatever is admirable—if anything is excellent or praiseworthy— **think about such things**. (Phil. 4:8)

Parents, tell your teen this story.

You've been chatting with a stranger for a few weeks. He seems like such a nice guy, but you start to get an uneasy feeling because of the direction he starts to take the conversation. Suddenly, you realize you've given out more information than you'd intended—and probably some you didn't even realize you gave—over the course of your chats. What do you do?

Now offer the following options with no personal commentary.

Let your teen think about the choices and make an honest decision.

A. You cut off all contact and delete the social profiles he knows about. You commit to safer online interaction in the future.

B. You're kind of nervous about pulling away completely. What if he gets mad? Or what if he really is a nice guy and you hurt his feelings? So you keep talking to him and try to keep things on a friends-only basis.

C. You realize that this is too big for you to deal with on your own and turn over all of the information and chat logs to your parents.

D. You call the police.

Crucial Step

Use this scenario to begin a discussion about online predators. Be very careful not to sound judgmental or accusatory. Remember, your teen is exploring thoughts and first impressions—these aren't actual choices . . .

yet. Mom and Dad, of course you're going to want your kids to follow the rules and avoid problems altogether, but you also need to make them feel safe in admitting they have made a mistake, so you can move forward to a solution together. (See part 4.)

Discussion Points

- Why did you make the choice you did?
- Safety is nothing to mess around with. Involve Mom and Dad.
- Make better choices by not getting into that situation.
- Pray that God will protect you from a situation like this.
- In a case like this, since you know you've given too much information, and you're feeling uncomfortable, it's best to allow Mom or Dad to contact someone who knows how to handle situations like this, such as the police.
- Chapter 8 discusses Internet predators and the statistics you should know.
- Do you now have a different view on this scenario than you did at the start? Why or why not?
- Would you like to change your answer or stick with it?

I called to **the LORD**, who **is worthy of praise**, and have been saved from my enemies.
(2 Sam. 22:4)

Parents, tell your teen this story.

One day after school you're in a chat room with a bunch of people your age. You know most of them, but not all. They're all sharing silly webcam pictures of themselves—nothing racy or cause for concern. Now it's your turn. They're waiting for you to play along. What do you do?

Now offer the following options with no personal commentary.

Let your teen think about the choices and make an honest decision.

> A. You're not allowed to post pictures online, so you ignore the requests.
> B. You post a very casual picture—nothing special. There's nothing to worry about anyway, since it's only your friends and kids your own age.
> C. You don't post the picture, but you offer to email it to a few of the chatters you trust.
> D. You leave the chat room immediately.

Crucial Step

Use this scenario to begin a discussion about the issue of sharing pictures online. Be very careful not to sound judgmental or accusatory. Remember, your teen is exploring thoughts and first impressions—these aren't actual choices . . . yet. Mom and Dad, if your teens are quick to say "I would never do that!" don't allow that to end the discussion. Press them to consider instances where they may let their guard down—when hanging out with

Christian friends, for instance—and then expose where the danger lies in that.

Discussion Points

- Why did you make the choice you did?
- What are your parents' rules?
- Why are those rules in place?
- You can't know for sure about strangers. They might not be who they say they are—fifty-fifty chance they aren't.
- There could also be anonymous lurkers you can't see.
- Predators are experts at finding minute details in photos. Things like photos on the walls behind you, what's visible out a window you're near, the license plate on the car you're leaning against—things you wouldn't think are revealing might give away your name and location.
- Emailing is worse. You give away your location unless you know how to hide your IP address.
- This is a game you can't win . . . so don't play.
- Read about social media in chapter 5.
- Do you now have a different view on this scenario than you did at the start? Why or why not?
- Would you like to change your answer or stick with it?

As obedient children, **do not conform to the evil desires** you had when you lived in ignorance. But just as he who called you is holy, **so be holy in all you do**; for it is written: "Be holy, because I am holy."

(1 Peter 1:14–16)

Parents, tell your teen this story.

Hey! Have you heard about this awesome site where people exchange all sorts of free stuff? You just post what you have to give away and what you're looking to find! It's awesome.

You've wanted a desk for your room for a long time, so you post on the site that you're looking for a wooden desk with drawers and a keyboard tray. White is preferable.

Ding.

Someone contacts you almost immediately to tell you he has the desk you're looking for and would be happy to give it to you for free. The only problem is that he has a back injury and can't bring it to you. He can help you get it in your car, but you'll need to go pick it up and only during the hours your parents are at work. What do you do?

Now offer the following options with no personal commentary.

Let your teen think about the choices and make an honest decision.

A. Thank him and ask your dad to help you find someone to go with you to get it.

B. Why can he help you get it in your car, but not deliver it? And why such a limited time frame? You tell him no thanks—you're kind of creeped out.

C. Go for it! Everyone else is using the site and no one seems to have any problem. A free desk—that's going to be great!

D. You drive by the house before you agree to pick it up, but you don't tell your parents, in case they tell you not to go.

Crucial Step

Use this scenario to begin a discussion about meeting people from online. Be very careful not to sound judgmental or accusatory. Remember, your teen is exploring thoughts and first impressions—these aren't actual choices . . . yet. Parents, consider, and then impress on your kids, the importance of personally accompanying them when they must face strangers. Don't just send them off with a buddy and assume there's "safety in numbers."

Discussion Points

- Why did you make the choice you did?
- There's a 50 percent chance it's a predator; there's no way to know who it really is.
- Girls are kidnapped and sold into sex trafficking this way.
- Predators find ways to identify with their victims: free desk.
- See chapter 8 to read about sex trafficking.
- There is the possibility that the giveaway is real. You need an adult to handle the situation for you.
- Do you now have a different view on this scenario than you did at the start? Why or why not?
- Would you like to change your answer or stick with it?

For **the LORD gives wisdom**; from his mouth come knowledge and understanding. (Prov. 2:6)

Parents, tell your teen this story.

You've been chatting with another guy you met at a Christian website. He's really nice—a Christian like you, and he also plays linebacker on his school's football team—just like you. He's coming to your town with his parents and wants to meet up with you. What do you do?

Now offer the following options with no personal commentary.

Let your teen think about the choices and make an honest decision.

> A. Sounds like fun! You agree to meet him. He's a guy and a Christian, so why not?
>
> B. You want to meet him and ask a parent to go with you. You make plans to meet at a public place and invite him to bring his parents.
>
> C. He might not even be who he says he is, and it's very unsafe to meet someone like that, so you say no.
>
> D. You arrange an opportunity for one of your parents to speak on the phone with one of his parents and let them organize a meeting opportunity if they think it's appropriate.

Crucial Step

Use this scenario to begin a discussion about making online friends. Be very careful not to sound judgmental or accusatory. Remember, your teen is exploring thoughts and first impressions—these aren't actual choices . . . yet. Mom and Dad, don't make the mistake of assuming that your sons are safer than your daughters when it comes to online predators.

Discussion Points

- Why did you make the choice you did?
- There's a 50 percent chance it's a predator; there's no way to know who it really is.
- Kids are kidnapped and sold into sex trafficking this way.
- Predators find ways to identify with their victims: boy, Christian, sports.
- There is the possibility that he's real—one way to find out would be to pass on meeting for this trip and see if you continue to hear from him. In this case, your parents need to make the call.
- Read about Internet predators in chapter 8.
- Do you believe this could happen to boys and to girls?
- Do you now have a different view on this scenario than you did at the start? Why or why not?
- Would you like to change your answer or stick with it?

To God belong **wisdom and power**; counsel and understanding **are his**.

(Job 12:13)

Parents, tell your teen this story.

Mom and Dad are out for the evening and you're bored. You decide to watch a movie, and since the television in Mom and Dad's room is way better than the one in your own room, you decide to go in there. Only there are no parental controls on their TV, and while you're flipping channels to decide what you want to watch, you stumble across images of two naked people doing all kinds of things you've never seen before. It looks interesting, but you know it's wrong to watch it. What do you do?

Now offer the following options with no personal commentary.

Let your teen think about the choices and make an honest decision.

> **A.** Turn off the TV and get out of there before someone comes home.
>
> **B.** Change the channel in a hurry, but tell your parents what you saw so they can explain it to you, and then put the controls on that TV too.
>
> **C.** Watch the show until you hear the garage door going up. You just want to know what the fuss is all about, after all. And maybe if you watch it, you won't be as tempted to do that stuff with your girlfriend or boyfriend.
>
> **D.** You assume your parents must be watching that stuff since they haven't bothered to block it, so why not watch it yourself?

Crucial Step

Use this scenario to begin a discussion about being on guard against the availability of pornography. Be very careful not to sound judgmental or accusatory. Remember, your teen is exploring thoughts and first impressions—these aren't actual choices . . . yet. Mom and Dad, consider the importance of open communication, no matter how embarrassing. Avoid the propensity toward judging curiosity, and just open the dialogue.

Discussion Points

- Why did you make the choice you did?
- You aren't responsible for what you accidentally see.
- Decide now to turn away immediately.
- You can't erase the images you see, so don't work around the filters and parental controls. They're there for a reason.
- If you have questions about sexuality, talk to your parents, not your friends. (Parents, for more on discussing matters of sexuality, see *Hot Buttons Sexuality Edition*.)
- Statistically it will make it harder to say no in the future.
- Go over the points about pornography in chapter 7.
- Protect your future marriage now by not defiling it with such things.
- Do you now have a different view on this scenario than you did at the start? Why or why not?
- Would you like to change your answer or stick with it?

Marriage should be honored by all, and the marriage bed **kept pure**, for God will judge the adulterer and all the sexually immoral. (Heb. 13:4)

Parents, tell your teen this story.

Your good friend has been pulling away from you lately. She rushes home from school every day to chat with a boy online. It's been going on for weeks and now he wants to meet her in person. You've told her that you don't think it's wise, but she trusts him because he's her age and says he goes to church every week. She plans to meet him next weekend at a local park, but promises she won't get into a car with him. What do you do?

Now offer the following options with no personal commentary.

Let your teen think about the choices and make an honest decision.

> A. You tell your parents the whole story and let them decide what to do.
> B. You offer to go with her. Two people are safer than one, and this way you avoid getting her into trouble while making sure she stays safe.
> C. You hope she knows what she's doing, but you stay out of it—after all, friends do support each other no matter what.
> D. You call the police.

Crucial Step

Use this scenario to begin a discussion about sex trafficking. Be very careful not to sound judgmental or accusatory. Remember, your teen is exploring thoughts and first impressions—these aren't actual choices . . . yet. Parents, the goal here is to create an open door of communication that leads your teens to make good choices for themselves, but also to look out for the safety and well-being of others.

Discussion Points

- Why did you make the choice you did?
- Again, it's a game you can't win, so don't play. Tell a parent.
- The likelihood that he's really who claims to be is so slim.
- What can that guy benefit from meeting a stranger online—is he not worthy of the girls he already knows in person?
- Staying out of it will make you responsible if something should happen.
- Be sure to tell a parent.
- It's not necessary to call the police immediately as there seems to be no imminent danger—as long as you turn the information over to a parent to handle.
- Chapter 8 deals with the topic of sex trafficking.
- Do you now have a different view on this scenario than you did at the start? Why or why not?
- Would you like to change your answer or stick with it?

The one **who gets wisdom loves life**; the one who cherishes understanding **will soon prosper**. (Prov. 19:8)

Parents, tell your teen this story. You've been hanging out with this super cool new math teacher. He's really been great to you and your buddies on the football team. One day, you're in his classroom after school hours, just killing time until practice. He pulls out his personal laptop and wants you to look at a website. You think nothing of it and glance over his shoulder. Turns out, it's a porn site with young boys.

Now offer the following options with no personal commentary.
Let your teen think about the choices and make an honest decision.

> **A.** You ask him to turn it off right away—you don't want to watch that because it makes you uncomfortable.
>
> **B.** You're afraid that if you get upset, he'll think you're going to tell someone. Just a few minutes won't hurt anything, and no one will know.
>
> **C.** You're horrified that he would do that, and you're disgusted at what you saw. You immediately go to the principal's office.
>
> **D.** Wow. You've heard about those movies, but have never actually seen one. You decide to check it out.

Crucial Step

Use this scenario to guide a discussion about pornography. Be very careful not to sound judgmental or accusatory. Remember, your teen is exploring thoughts and first impressions—these aren't actual choices . . . yet. Mom and Dad, you might stumble onto discussions with your teen of a more graphic sexual nature with this scenario. Don't panic. Just be honest.

Discussion Points

- Why did you make the choice you did?
- Do you know what a pedophile is?
- What did the teacher do wrong?
- The Internet is often used as a tool to introduce unsuspecting teens to porn and deviant sexual behaviors.
- Discuss boundaries and what to do if a situation with a trusted adult grows uncomfortable.
- Be on guard against adults who spend a lot of time befriending teenagers.
- Chapter 8 has a lot of information on the topic of pornography. Refer to it as necessary.
- Do you now have a different view on this scenario than you did at the start? Why or why not?
- Would you like to change your answer or stick with it?

Be on your guard;

stand firm

in the faith;

be courageous;

be strong.

(1 Cor. 16:13)

PART FOUR

Parent-Teen STUDY GUIDE

Congratulations on making it this far through *Hot Buttons Internet Edition*! This book has dealt with some tough issues and walked you through the practice of using Strategic Scenarios to prepare your family. Now we're going to press in a little deeper and do some work on the spiritual side of choices, sin, confession, and forgiveness. No matter what the ages of your children are, you'll find some common ground and will learn something about each other through these studies.

As lines of communication open, and awareness deepens through the use of the Strategic Scenarios, pray for guidance as to the right time to go through these studies. I hesitate to write a formula that tells you precisely when that is, because each family situation is different. I'd rather leave the timing up to the guidance of the Holy Spirit. But when you do, I recommend that you work through these studies individually, then come together to discuss your findings.

Visit www.hotbuttonsite.com to find a downloadable and printable version of this study guide in which space for writing is included, so everyone can have a copy for personal study.

Confession

Very **truly I tell you**, the one who ***believes*** has eternal life. (John 6:47)

. . . **Jesus is the Messiah**, the Son of God, and that **by *believing*** you may have life in his name. (John 20:31)

Jesus said to her, "I am the resurrection and the life. The one **who *believes* in me will live**, even though they die; and whoever lives by believing in me will never die. Do you *believe* this?" (John 11:25–26)

If you **confess with your mouth Jesus as Lord**, and ***believe* in your heart** that God raised Him from the dead, **you will be saved**; for with the heart a person *believes*, resulting in righteousness, and with the mouth he confesses, resulting in salvation. (Rom. 10:9–10 NASB)

◀ According to these verses, what is required for salvation?

Stop and think. Have you confessed with your mouth and believed in your heart that Jesus is Lord? Share the answer with your study partner(s).

◀ What does that mean to you to have made that choice?

If you haven't done that but would like to now, take a walk through the following Scriptures. If you're a Christian already, it's still a good exercise to look at these foundational truths as a refresher.

◀ Read Romans 3:23. Who has sinned?

◀ Read Romans 6:23a. What is the price of sin?

Sin requires a penalty. The only payment for it is death, blood. Worse than a physical death, though, is the spiritual death that separates us from God for eternity.

◀ Read Romans 6:23b. What is God's gift?

◀ Read Romans 5:8. How much does God love you?

Jesus gave His own life on the cross to pay the penalty for all of our sin. He, an innocent man, took your death sentence and stood in your place, giving you new life in exchange for His death.

◀ Read Romans 10:13 and Revelation 3:20. Who qualifies for salvation?

If you'd like to welcome Jesus into your life and receive the free gift of eternal life that He offers, simply pray this prayer:

Dear Jesus, I believe in You. I believe that You are the Son of God and my Savior and Lord. I ask You to forgive my sins and make me clean. Please help me do the right thing, but I thank You for the forgiveness You offer me when I mess up. I give my life to You. Amen.

If you took that step, *congratulations*!

Everything pales in comparison to the choice to walk with Jesus through your life. Now we can apply that choice of confession to the issues in this book and to your relationships.

> Therefore **confess your sins** to each other and pray for each other so that you may be healed. The **prayer of a righteous person is powerful** and effective. (James 5:16)

Confessing your sins *to others* is not a requirement of salvation. James 5 doesn't suggest that you should confess your sins to each other so that you might be saved. Confession to God is the only path to salvation. James 5 is referring instead to healing of the mind, the mending of broken trust, and the repairing of damaged relationships that only comes about by seeking forgiveness from those you have wronged in the past.

Confession clears the air and allows forgiveness to blossom where bitterness once festered. And confession carries healing power no matter what the response is. In other words, your confession starts the healing process in you, regardless of how it's received or if forgiveness is immediately granted.

◀Work together to write a description of the purpose of confession in family relationships.

Though forgiveness in Christ is complete, sin continues to thrive in the darkness of secrecy. Confession to a loved one deflates sin's power like the air rushing out of a balloon. The sin shrivels, its grip releases, and its power dies. What was once a tool of the enemy to destroy you and your family is now a bonding agent that unites and builds strength and character. What a victory!

When is it important to confess to each other?

- ◀ When the issue is causing division
- ◀ When there is bitterness
- ◀ When you're unable to find peace
- ◀ When you need forgiveness

Now is the time to take a risk. You've confessed to God, and you're forgiven of your sins because of the death and resurrection of God's Son, Jesus. Now it's time to lay your heart bare before your loved ones. Trust that we'll get to the forgiveness part of this study just as soon as you turn the page. Let go of the fear of admitting your faults. Confess today so you can be forgiven and see your relationships restored once and for all.

Open your heart and mind, and let the Holy Spirit reveal the things that you need to let out. Let this be a safe moment in your family in which you feel free to lay your heart bare and free your spirit of any guilt or condemnation that binds you.

◀Take this time to confess whatever the Lord is bringing to your mind. You may verbalize your confession, or write it in your own notebook or in your study guide (which you can find at www.hotbuttonsite.com).

Trust that your loved ones' response to your confession will be one of forgiveness—the next chapter will lead you through that.

Parent's Prayer

Father, I confess the times I've failed as a parent and ask You to forgive me and help me have more self-control and wisdom when I respond to things. Please help me to be a godly example and a role model for my kids. Give us the kind of relationship that mirrors the one You have with us. Thank You for Your example of unconditional love, continual acceptance, and constant approachability. Make me that kind of parent, and help my family to forgive me for the times I haven't been. Amen.

Teen's Prayer

Dear God, please forgive me for not respecting my parents all the time. Help me to honor the values we've decided upon as a family and uphold them in all things. Give me the strength to say no to the pressure I'm placed under to do all sorts of wrong things. Please help me to be a better son/daughter and make us a loving and united family that serves You together. Amen.

13 Forgiveness

Following belief and confession is forgiveness. Ah, what a blessed state to live in . . . forgiven. The very word elicits a sense of peace and calm. It inspires me to take a deep breath and rest for a moment in gratitude.

How about you? Do you feel forgiven?

> If we **confess our sins**, he is faithful and just and will **forgive us** our sins and **purify us** from all unrighteousness. (1 John 1:9)

Do you believe that you're forgiven? Sometimes it hits like a tsunami as the waves of peace wash over the heart. For others, it's more of a steady rain that takes time to feel. It's okay, either way. Whether you feel forgiven or not, you can have faith that you are, in fact, purified and holy before God.

So God has forgiven you, but now what does He expect you to do about other people who have wronged you?

For if you **forgive other people** when they sin against you, your **heavenly Father will also forgive you**. But if you do not forgive others their sins, your Father will not forgive your sins. (Matt. 6:14–15)

◄ What does that verse teach about forgiveness?

◄ How do you feel about that?

Forgiving others is often a simple act of obedience and a step of faith. If you're angry or wronged in some way, you're rarely going to feel like forgiving those who hurt you. Forgiveness, in that case, is a gift from God planted in your heart so that you might extend it toward those who sinned against you.

Would you be surprised if I told you that offering forgiveness benefits you far more than it benefits the person you're attempting to forgive? Surrendering in that way allows God to work more deeply in your life.

◄ Read Ephesians 4:25 and Luke 15. How do you think God wants us to receive someone's confession?

◄ Now, think about this question: Can you truly accept someone's confession and offer forgiveness without holding on to any bitterness or contempt?

◄ What makes that easy or difficult for you?

◄ Read Matthew 18:21–35. Who do the characters in this parable represent? What is the debt? What is the parable trying to show us?

> **Bear with each another** and forgive one another if any of you has a grievance against someone. **Forgive as the Lord forgave you**. And over all these virtues put on love, which binds them **all together in perfect unity**. (Col. 3:13–14)

Parents, name some times you've been forgiven of things in your life and share them here. Try for at least five examples. Spend as much time thinking about this as necessary.

When you see it written out like that, does it give you a different perspective on your teen's sins?

But I'm not God!

What about when it's just too bad, and I'm truly unable to let go of the anger toward someone?

> And when you stand praying, if you hold anything against anyone, **forgive him**, so that your Father in heaven may forgive you your sins. (Mark 11:25)

> Do not judge, and you will not be judged. Do not condemn, and you will not be condemned. **Forgive**, and you will be forgiven. (Luke 6:37)

Believe me, I get it. It's not easy to forgive those who have committed a painful wrong against you and are truly guilty. The problem is that unforgiveness drives a wedge into our daily walk with God. That free and open walk with a loving Savior becomes strained and even avoided when your spirit knows it's harboring something God cannot abide. He talked to His children about this specific issue because He doesn't want it to divide you from Him.

◀ Are you able to forgive each other for the things confessed before God in the last chapter? Are you able to treat those confessions with the same manner of grace that God has shown you? Is anything standing in your way? Take turns sharing.

We've made huge progress through confessing to God and each other, receiving God's grace, and forgiving others. I'd like to encourage you to backtrack a little and dig a little deeper.

◀ What are you still holding on to that needs to be confessed to your family? What sin still makes you cringe when you consider sharing it? Why can't you let it go?

Now's the time to take a chance. Forgiveness is a step away. Families, assure each other that it's safe to unload anything at this time. God has forgiven your sins, past, present, and future—now allow your family to do the same.

Confession followed by forgiveness is a life-changing gift of healing.

Parent's Prayer

Heavenly Father, I'm so grateful for Your grace and forgiveness. I'm so grateful that it extends to cover the mistakes I make as a Christian and as a parent. Please help me forgive others like You have forgiven me so that I can be an extension of Your arm of mercy to those around me. Let me show grace to my children so they will trust me with their sins and their feelings. Help me not to expect them to be perfect, but rather to see them as You see them and readily offer forgiveness at all times. Amen.

Teen's Prayer

Lord, I've done some dumb things—thank You for forgiving me for them. Your gift of salvation has changed my life, and I'm not the same person I was before You came into it. Thank You, too, for helping me and my family work through some of these things. It all makes sense when we talk about it and look at what the Bible says. Help me not to hold grudges against people who have hurt me, and help me to be obedient to You and to my parents. Please help me make good decisions and not to give in to peer pressure. Amen.

Clean Slate **14**

For as **high as the heavens** are above the earth,
so great is his love for those who fear him;
as far as the east is from the west,
so far has he **removed our transgressions** from us.
(Ps. 103:11–12)

◀ In light of Psalm 103:11–12, what does the following quote mean to you?

> "I can forgive, but I cannot forget," is only another way of saying, "I will not forgive." Forgiveness ought to be like a cancelled note, torn in two, and burned up so it can never be shown against one.   —Henry Ward Beecher

Confession + Forgiveness = Perfection   . . . *right?*

Unfortunately, I think we all know it doesn't quite work that way. The question I receive at this point in the discussion goes something like this:

"So, if I continue to mess up and the people I've forgiven continue to mess up, how can we live with a clean slate?"

◀ Read Romans 7:14–20. What does Paul do? What is he unable to do? Why is he unable to do it?

Paul is a believer. He's forgiven. He's a mighty servant of God, yet he sins. He wants to do what is right, but he often cannot. He doesn't want to do wrong, but often cannot stop himself.

◀ Continue on by reading Romans 7:21–25.

No matter how committed you are to a clean slate, your enemy, the devil, wants nothing more than to sabotage forgiveness, trust, and peace. He is the antithesis of the love you feel for each other and will stop at nothing to erode it.

There are three steps to combat the devil's attacks.

◀ Read James 4:6–8.

Step One: _____ the devil.

What does that mean to you?

What are some ways to do that as it relates to the subject of this book?

◀ Read Luke 6:27 and Acts 7:54–60.

Step Two: _____ your enemies. _____ for those who have mistreated you.

What does that mean to you?

What are some ways to do that as it relates to the issues you've been addressing with the Strategic Scenarios?

◀ Reread James 4:6–8.

Step Three: _____ _____ to God and He will _____ _____ to you.

What does that mean to you?

What are some ways to do that as it relates to the hot-button issues you've been addressing?

Immerse yourself in Scripture and prayer to counter the devil's attacks.

Romans 7 (that we looked at above) ends with a description of the battle between Paul's sin nature and his commitment to God. Good ol' Paul admits that he messes up all the time. But we know that, even though he claimed to be at war with the flesh and struggling with sin, he found favor with God. Let's take a look at Romans 8:1–4 to see the resolution:

> Therefore, **there is now no condemnation** for those who are in Christ Jesus, because through Christ Jesus the law of the Spirit who gives life has **set you free from the law of sin** and death. For what the law was powerless to do because it was weakened by the flesh, God did by **sending his own Son in the likeness of sinful flesh** to be a sin offering. And so he condemned sin in the flesh, in order that the righteous requirement of the law might be fully met in us, who do not live according to the flesh but according to the Spirit.

We have a clean slate before God. It's His promise to us in response to the work of His Son, Jesus. With the slate wiped clean for us, we are able to do the same for others. We're all a work in progress; not a single one of us is perfected and complete. We're complete in Jesus—because of Him—but not because of anything we've done. So allow others the same grace of being "in progress" that your heavenly Father is showing you by keeping your slate free from judgment.

> Being confident of this, that he who **began a good work in you** will carry it on to completion **until the day of Christ Jesus**. (Phil. 1:6)

◀ We looked at Philippians 1:6 back in chapter 3, but let's break it down again. Describe what the phrases in the verse mean to you.

Being confident of this

That He who began

A good work in you

Will carry it on to completion

Until the day of Christ Jesus

◀ How can you apply those truths to yourself and your clean slate before God?

◀ How about others and their slate before you? Is it clean in your eyes? Can you forgive an imperfect person?

From that verse, we're reminded that no one is perfect—we're all a work in progress. Commit to forgiving the failures of others, since you know that you will fail and others will forgive you.

The best way to preempt disappointment is to communicate needs and expectations. Each of you, take a moment to share three needs you have regarding the hot-button issues you've been addressing. For example: "More understanding and space when I'm in a bad mood." I recommend you put this list in writing so there's no confusion later.

Parent Commitments

Speak these commitments out loud to your teen(s):

- ◖ I commit to do my best to be a godly example.
- ◖ I commit to having an open mind and heart, ready to listen whenever you need to talk.
- ◖ I commit to being humble enough to admit when I'm wrong, but strong enough to enforce the boundaries I believe are necessary.
- ◖ I commit to _____.
  [fill in the blank based on the needs communicated above]
- ◖ I commit to _____.
  [fill in the blank based on the needs communicated above]
- ◖ I commit to _____.
  [fill in the blank based on the needs communicated above]

Sign: _____

Date: _____

Teen Commitments

Speak these commitments out loud to your parent(s).

- ◀ I commit to do my best to follow your example and do what's right, including being honest at all times.

- ◀ I commit to having an open mind to try to understand that what you ask and expect of me is for my own good.

- ◀ I commit to being humble enough to admit when I'm wrong and honest about how I feel.

- ◀ I commit to _____.
  [fill in the blank based on the needs communicated above]

- ◀ I commit to _____.
  [fill in the blank based on the needs communicated above]

- ◀ I commit to _____.
  [fill in the blank based on the needs communicated above]

Sign: _____

Date: _____

Remember that your enemy, the devil, seeks to sabotage forgiveness, trust, and peace. It's so easy to stumble down a slippery slope.

The pattern of confession, forgiveness, and a clean slate is perfectly portrayed in the relationship you have with your heavenly Father. He loves you, and wants you to walk in complete forgiveness, confident in His love for you. He also wants you to experience that love in your family.

People fail—they've failed you before, and they'll fail you again. You can't wait for God to perfect those you love, but you can allow His perfect love to cover a multitude of sins—grace from Him to you, and through you to them.

> May God himself, **the God of peace**, sanctify you through and through. May your whole spirit, soul and body **be kept blameless** at the coming of our Lord Jesus Christ. The one who calls you is faithful, and **he will do it**. (1 Thess. 5:23–24)

My Prayer for You

Heavenly Father, I lift this family up to You and thank You for their precious hearts that desire to grow closer together. Please guide them as they join hands and walk together in a united purpose to serve You throughout their lives. Facing these Hot Buttons involves release and trust. Help Mom and Dad to use wisdom in knowing when and how to begin the process of that kind of release, and help the teens to respect the boundaries set by the parents and by Your Word. Give them wisdom and strength when it comes to the choices they must make in life. Grant them Your holy sight to see down the road when the way is unclear to them. Help them also to trust each other with some of the tough decisions. As the years go by, remind them of the things they talked about in this book and the commitments they've made to each other. Give them joy as they embark on life with a clean slate. Amen.

Parent's Prayer

Father, I thank You for my family—they're perfect in Your eyes. Help me to take joy in them each and every day—just like You do. You've given us the gift of a clean slate in Your eyes . . . help us to walk in that freedom with each other too. Help me love my family like You do—unconditionally and unselfishly. Please give me wisdom and patience as I help my teens wade through these years. Amen.

Teen's Prayer

Dear Jesus, thank You for forgiveness and for a clean slate. Thank You for a family who wants to serve You and will work hard to make sure I'm on the right path. Please give me wisdom in all things, especially the choices I have to make about these hot-button issues. Help me to do the right thing and to have the strength to stand up to the pressures of life. Amen.

Recommended
Resources

Books

Arterburn, Stephen, and Roger Marsh. *Internet-Protect Your Kids: Keep Your Children Safe from the Dark Side of Technology.* Nashville: Thomas Nelson, 2007.

Courtney, Vicki. *Logged On and Tuned Out: A Non-Techie's Guide to Parenting a Tech-Savvy Generation.* Nashville: B&H Publishing, 2007.

Stocker, Todd, with Nathan Stocker. *Infinite Playlists: How to Have Conversations (Not Conflict) with Your Kids About Music.* Grand Rapids: Kregel, 2010.

Filters

Bsecure Online is the Internet filter and online security software program endorsed by Focus on the Family since 2011.

FamilyFellowship.com is a home Internet filtering system with a Christian perspective and an accountability program.

SafeEyes, a Christian Internet filter, is recommended by Men of Integrity and Dave Ramsey.

Total Net Guard is a Christian Internet filter.

True Vine is a Christian Internet filter owned and serviced by Christians.

Websites

www.chooseNOWradio.com. The home of *Parent Talk* and *Teen Talk*, where Nicole O'Dell talks with guests about issues teens and their parents need to know about. Topics like peer pressure, dating, body image, self-esteem, friendships, entertainment, and anything else that comes up are covered in a fun, casual environment.

www.choose-NOW.com. The Internet home of Nicole O'Dell and Choose NOW Ministries, dedicated to battling peer pressure by tackling the tough issues and bridging the gap in parent-teen communication.

www.familylife.com. Committed to helping people know and apply the biblical blueprints for maintaining a God-honoring marriage and raising children to become responsible adults. Created on the principle that the family provides the foundation for society, the ministry offers a wide range of tools to help families become stronger.

www.focusonthefamily.com. A global Christian ministry dedicated to helping families thrive. They provide help and resources for couples to build healthy marriages that reflect God's design, and for parents to raise their children according to morals and values grounded in biblical principles.

Recommended Resources

www.findlaw.com. As mentioned previously in this book, individual state laws regarding child pornography can be found here: http://law.findlaw .com/state-laws/child-pornography.

www.hotbuttonsite.com. The Internet home of the Hot Buttons column, where Nicole O'Dell regularly brings you new Hot Buttons scenarios free of charge, for you to use to foster healthy, proactive communication in your family.

www.sharedhope.org. Shared Hope International exists to rescue and restore women and children in crisis. They are leaders in a worldwide effort to prevent and eradicate sex trafficking and slavery through education and public awareness.

www.shoutlife.com. A free and family-friendly social networking site that offers profiles, blogging, instant messaging, and more.

Notes

1. Grunwald Associates, "Two Million American Children Have Their Own Web Sites, Broad New Internet Survey Shows," December 4, 2003, http://www.grunwald.com/reports/cfi/news release.php.

2. Samuel McQuade III and Neel Sampat, "Survey of Internet and At-Risk Behaviors," Report of the Rochester Institute of Technology, June 18, 2008, http://www.rrcsei.org/RIT%20Cyber %20Survey%20Final%20Report.pdf.

3. Symantec Corporation, "Symantec Survey Finds Kids Outsmart Parents When It Comes to the Internet," August 9, 2007, http://www.symantec.com/about/news/release/article.jsp?prid= 20070809_01.

4. Kaiser Family Foundation, "Daily Media Use Among Children and Teens Up Dramatically from Five Years Ago," January 20, 2010, http://www.kff.org/entmedia/entmedia012010nr.cfm.

5. Cox Communications, "Cox Communications Teen Internet Safety Survey, Wave II—in Partnership with the National Center for Missing and Exploited Children (NCMEC) and John Walsh," March 2007, http://ww2.cox.com/wcm/en/aboutus/datasheet/

takecharge/archives/2007-teen-survey.pdf?campcode=takecharge
-archive-link_2007-survey_0511.

6. Ibid.

7. "Creating & Connecting: Research and Guidelines on Online Social
and Educational Networking," National School Boards Association,
July 2007, http://www.nsba.org/Services/TLN/BenefitsofMembership/
Publications/Creating-and-Connecting.pdf.

8. Kelly Pfeiffer, "Are Social Networking Sites Unhealthy for Teens?: Studies
Reveal How Facebook & MySpace Affect Relationship Skills," February
7, 2010, http://www.suite101.com/content/are-social-networking-sites
-unhealthy-for-teens-a199105#ixzz1IZYUxJYA.

9. Trish Van Pilsum with Fox 9 Investigators, "Is Formspring a New
Forum for Bullying?" February 16, 2011, http://www.myfoxtwincities.
com/dpp/news/scitech/is-formspring-a-new-forum-for-bullying%3F
-feb-16-2011.

10. Cox Communications, "Cox Communications Teen Internet Safety
Survey, Wave II—in Partnership with the National Center for Missing and Exploited Children (NCMEC) and John Walsh," March 2007,
http://ww2.cox.com/wcm/en/aboutus/datasheet/takecharge/archives
/2007-teen-survey.pdf?campcode=takecharge-archive-link_2007
-survey_0511.

11. Top Ten Reviews, "Internet Filter Software Review," http://internet
-filter-review.toptenreviews.com (accessed January 2012).

12. Samuel McQuade III and Neel Sampat, "Survey of Internet and At-
Risk Behaviors," Report of the Rochester Institute of Technology, June
18, 2008, http://www.rrcsei.org/RIT%20Cyber%20Survey%20Final%
20Report.pdf.

13. Ibid.

14. NewsMax.com, "42 Percent Of Kids, Teens View Porn Online," February 2, 2007, http://archive.newsmax.com/archives/ic/2007/2/5/112124 .shtml?s=ic.

15. Jerry Ropelato, "Internet Pornography Statistics," Top Ten Reviews, http://internet-filter-review.toptenreviews.com/internet-pornography -statistics.html (accessed January 2012).

16. Catey Hill, "Study: Teens Spend 87 Hours Per Year Looking at Online Porn," Daily News, February 10, 2009, http://www.nydailynews.com/ news/money/study-teens-spend-87-hours-year-online-porn-article -1.389603#ixzzljyb3Y1k8.

17. Judith Newman, "Parent Alert: Teens and Porn," *Reader's Digest*, May 2009, http://www.rd.com/family/parent-alert-teens-and-porn/.

18. *Tampa Bay Times*, "Teenager Pleads Guilty to Possession of Child Porn, Becomes Sex Offender," April 9, 2010, http://www.tampabay. com/news/courts/criminal/teenager-pleads-guilty-to-possession-of -child-porn-becomes-sex-offender/1086012.

19. The Federal Bureau of Investigation, "Keeping Kids Safe Online," January 11, 2011, http://www.fbi.gov/news/stories/2011/january/online_ 011111/online_011111.

20. Perverted Justice, chat log of Maurice Wolin, Piedmont, CA, April 30, 2010, http://www.perverted-justice.com/?con=talldreamy_doc. Used by permission.

21. Perverted Justice, "Real Stories Project," May 25, 2010, http://www .perverted-justice.com/?stories=321.

22. Perverted Justice, "Real Stories Project," May 22, 2010, http://www .perverted-justice.com/?stories=318.

23. Chris Hansen, "Catching Potential Internet Sex Predators," *Dateline NBC*, November 10, 2005, http://www.msnbc.msn.com/id/9927253/.

24. The Federal Bureau of Investigation, "Keeping Kids Safe Online," January 11, 2011, http://www.fbi.gov/news/stories/2011/january/online_011111/online_011111.

25. Janis Wolak et al., "Online 'Predators' and Their Victims," *American Psychologist* 63, no. 2 (Feb–Mar 2008): 112, doi:10.1037/0003-066X.63.2.111.

26. Shared Hope International, "The National Report on Domestic Minor Sex Trafficking," 2009, http://www.sharedhope.org/Portals/0/Documents/BrowardandDadeFlorida_printerfirendly.pdf.

27. Heather Sells, "Sex Trade: Innocence Lost in America's Heartland," CBN News, June 14, 2010, http://www.cbn.com/cbnnews/us/2010/March/Sex-Trade-Innocence-Lost-in-Americas-Heartland-/.

28. FBI, "Cyber Alerts for Parents & Kids," December 22, 2011, http://www.fbi.gov/news/stories/2011/december/cyber_122211/cyber_122211.

About the
Author

Youth culture expert **Nicole O'Dell** resides in Paxton, Illinois, with her husband and six children—the youngest of whom are toddler triplets. She's the founder of Choose NOW Ministries, dedicated to battling peer pressure and guiding teens through tough issues while helping parents encourage good decisions, and the host of Choose NOW Radio: Parent Talk and Teen Talk, where "It's all about choices!"

A full-time author of both fiction and nonfiction, Nicole's desire is to bridge the gap between parents and teens. Her popular Scenarios for Girls series, the natural segue into the Hot Buttons series, asks teen readers to make tough choices for the main characters and offers alternate endings based on the individual reader's choices.

For more information on Nicole's books or to schedule her for a speaking event or interview, visit www.nicoleodell.com. Follow @Hot_Buttons on Twitter, and like www.facebook.com/HotButtons. Podcasts of *Choose NOW Radio* are available at www.chooseNOWradio.com.